19.99

Come Into My Life
Introducing Love Relationship Therapy

3 8/8

H. Dale Zimmerman, M. Div, Ed. D.

Charming Forge Publishing and Artworks
Robesonia, Pennsylvania

i

Come Into My Life

© 1994 by H. Dale Zimmerman

Requests for information should be addressed to:
Charming Forge Publishing and Artworks
Box 190, R.D. 1
Robesonia, PA 19551

Printed in the United States of America
by Reading Eagle Press

Published by Charming Forge Publishing and Artworks
Box 190, R.D. 1
Robesonia, PA 19551

ISBN: 1-884768-02-4
Library of Congress Catalog Card Number 93-74875

To all husbands and wives now, and those yet to become, who are committed to a relationship of love.

All names appearing in this book have been changed and, in some case illustrations, descriptive facts have been altered to protect the privacy and confidentiality of individuals with whom the author had shared a privileged relationship.

CONTENTS

Contents

ACKNOWLEDGMENTS

I thank all the husbands and wives who invited me into their relationships where I could observe the many faces of love. Love cannot be learned from a definition. We know love only by experiencing love. As these couples experienced their growing love, I carefully studied each of its kaleidoscopic reflections which their changing relationships brought into view. I was, in a very real way, their student in love's classroom.

Richard Morrison spent many hours helping me shape the manuscript into its final form. I owe him my deepest appreciation. His editorial assistance gave clearer understanding to the formative ideas used to develop the thesis of this book.

The jacket for this book, designed by David Bullock, captures the essence of a love relationship in a way that words cannot do. I'm fortunate to have been able to have the benefit of his artistic skills and creative thoughtfulness.

A special note of thanks goes to Charlotte and Wesley Bahorik, very dear friends, whose review of the original text and kindly counsel and selective editing ushered me into the phase of publication that takes an author from the tedious work of writing to the excitement of printing and production. Their enthusiasm lifted my languishing spirit that came from years of laboring to frame the concepts for this book and write them into its final form.

A special thanks to my son and colleague, Jeffrey Zimmerman, for his technical assistance in planning the book's format and for "walking with me" through the development of the many concepts that form the foundation for love relationship therapy. His suggestions were most insightful, filling in many of the details that my general style of focusing tends to miss.

But most of all, to my beloved wife, Norma, I say, "Thank you for all the love you gave me through the years. It was your love that proved to me how the power of love alone surmounts all obstacles on the journey to a committed and affectionate relationship."

Preface

From the moment we rise in the morning until we go to bed at night we cross people's paths. Leaving the bedroom, our spouse or child greets us. By day's end our lives intertwine with those of countless other people, by choice or by chance. Our relationships may be pleasant, contentious, or dutifully shared.

We relate so routinely that we don't think about the *bonding mechanisms* that bring us together. We are concerned only with the practical, personal, or emotional satisfactions we get from relating. And when we don't get satisfaction, we blame others for not responding to us in ways we expected.

We're unhappy with relationships that don't fulfill our needs. The bond that keeps us in relationships is the need it satisfies. And the type of need determines the type of bond holding us together in a relationship. *One scenario:* a television reporter relating the sordid details of a family physician accused of sexually violating a female patient. *Another scenario:* a 90-year-old family doctor whose life was presented as a human interest story to close out a weekly television news program. She was the only woman, and the only surviving doctor from her medical school graduating class in the 1930's. Video taping showed a loving, kind person, tenderly comforting a child and empathically hearing the concerns of her adult patients. She embodied human compassion.

We have two physicians, but with clearly different objectives. One breaks his oath and is a defendant in a law suit. The other is revered for her saintly love. The woman who is treated impersonally and unethically by her male physician comes out of her relationship feeling bitter and vengeful. All the patients of the female physician relate to her with endearing warmth and gratitude.

What makes the difference? We can't answer this question just by looking at the outcomes of their relationships. Rather, the difference is in the bond that unites the doctors to their patients. For the one physician the bond is *service to self*, and for the other it is generous *giving of self*.

The patients' need in both situations is to become physically well. The need of one physician is to exploit a woman for personal pleasure. The need of the other physician is to provide the medicine of healing, to be professionally fulfilled and, in some measure, to be monetarily rewarded. This example, illustrates how we understand relationships only by knowing the needs that bind people in them.

Every day many people invite us into their lives or life spaces. Or we ask them to come into ours. The commercial world says to us, "Come to our grand opening ...take advantage of our giant inventory ...don't miss our one-time sale ...use our easy credit plan." Friends invite us into their homes. Men and women ask each other for dates and, if their relationships flower, they propose marriage. And little children say to one another, "Come out and play with me."

Come Into My Life is an invitation we receive in one form or another several times daily. Each invitation that we accept leads to a relationship that eventually is pleasing or displeasing. It pleases if it fulfills our expectations and displeases when it does not.

When we don't receive what we desire from relationships, we become angry and turn against those whom we feel have failed to provide benefits we expected. So we know by its outcome if a relationship is good or bad, and whether we want to remain in it or to withdraw. Usually we do not analyze relationships to determine why they have been rewarding or unrewarding. If we did, we would discover in every case that the person with whom we were relating either used the same bond we used - hence, a rewarding relationship - or a different bond and, thus, an unrewarding relationship.

Although I provide in this book detailed descriptions of the total range of relationships, and of the bonds that create them, my primary focus is on "love-bonded" relationships. Easy access to divorce invites men and women to sever their bonds when relationships weaken. Marriages, for half of all couples, become little more than revolving doors. They have little sanctity, and certainly are not the "honorable estate" proclaimed in marriage ceremonies. They are entered into without commitments and often terminated with few regrets. They cannot survive because the partners do not unite with the type of bond that is strong enough to bear the full weight of the burdens that naturally accompany intimate relating.

Social researchers frequently conduct surveys to determine what attracts men and women to each other. Answers given by many women describe men who are fun-loving, good looking, successful, hard-working, intelligent, outgoing, and charming. *Yet, when women marry men with some or all of these traits, and later have conflicts in their marriages, they fault their husbands for failing to display an entirely different set of characteristics: being thoughtful, tender, compassionate, giving, kind, considerate and devoted.*

Clearly, this second group of traits describes people who place others in the center of their lives. The first set of traits, on the other hand, describes people who tend to live in the center of their own lives. What kind of a relationship, therefore, would we expect two individuals from the same group to have with each other? What type of a bond, and what kind of a relationship would a person from each group have with the other? Scant consideration is given to these questions when two persons, "in love," decide to enter each other's life.

Too often, couples begin to examine their relationships and marriages only after years of unhappy and contentious living together. Usually they ask professional counselors to help with these examinations. In most instances, unfortunately, counselors and clients alike consider only the disagreements and ignore the forces that cause them. If they were to look for causes, they would find them within the bond that unites husbands and wives in their relationships.

Counselors can't give meaningful assistance to couples in troubled marriages by simply negotiating conflicts. They must help them identify and analyze their interactions and the needs they fulfill. They must help them understand the power of these needs, and how they determine and control their behavior. Above all, they must lead them through an honest scrutiny of the real purposes of their relationships. When couples do this, they find that their bonds of personal "need satisfaction" are stronger than the bonds of "selfless love."

Therapy should focus, then, not on interpersonal clashes, but on the bonds and how these bonds hold couples together through their unyielding domination over their relationships. This therapy traces the origin of marital dissension to the acting out of the "ego's" mandate, "me before you" or "you after me."

In *Come Into My Life*, I present a framework for understanding marital disharmony as a function of defective bonding. It offers an alternative approach to behavioral systems that most marriage counselors now use. Further, I show that reconciliation can include a spiritual revitalization of two people in their *union of one*, though not with all the romantic and emotional trimmings traditionally associated with "being in love." Although marriages can't always be sustained in the excitement of romance, they don't have to take on the monotony of routine and boredom. With the use of love-bonding, marriages need not become labored commitments. They can be a joyful devotion of self in love to another.

Introduction

Increasingly, the American family is becoming a broken institution, declining in importance in the lives of its members - parents and children. Family counselors, television talk show hosts, religious leaders, school teachers, community leaders, and, in the 1990's, politicians, lament the passing of the traditional family with its role of teaching and nurturing the values upon which stable lives and a stable society depend.

Who is to blame for the collapse of the family, this assault on the time-honored and durable fortress that has been the bulwark of our society? I think we all agree that the family, in its weakened condition, lacks the resolve to defend itself against the corrupting influences that are rapidly changing family values: materialism and the enslavement to pleasure; the modeling of celebrities who ridicule the "old fashioned" ideas about family; drug and alcohol abuse; liberalization of sexual behaviors; laws stripping parents of authority over their children; removing religion from schools and public life; and the failure of clergy to forthrightly denounce sexual immorality and to preach the morality of marital commitment and fidelity. These attacks on families undermine the loyalties of its members. Divide and conquer, an old tactic, still works.

Compared to these commonly recognized ills, a subtler foe of traditional family relationships is the marriage and family counselor. Trained predominately in the "family systems" model, they contribute to the demise of the family spirit and the flow of loving relationships by promoting togetherness without the blending of compassionate and tender devotion.

True, when the family counselor is successful, a troubled family may remain intact. However, the members don't get inside the embraces of one another's affection. They don't fold each other to their hearts. Husband and wife co-labor in the management of their household with the emotional detachment of business partners united only by practical interest and need. Their children mirror the same passionless connections with one another and with their parents.

During the last 30 years we have witnessed an explosive increase in the number of persons "hanging out their shingles" to do marriage counseling. This growth coincides with the movement to advance women's rights and growing tension between the sexes. The twin offspring of this socially unsettling change is escalating divorce rates and a dramatic restructuring of the family. These social changes affect millions of lives, leaving people confused and drifting aimlessly in a quest for happiness - a goal they have difficulty defining. Thus, they turn more and more to professional counselors for help to regain stability and direction for living. Counseling is needed. And this need has further fueled an increase in practitioners. But this increase has, unfortunately, been in specialty areas, many of which cannot provide the full range of services clients require. Some of the interest areas in which these counselors specialize are: balancing career and family, battered wives, child abuse and sexual molestation, inter-racial marriage, women's issues, blended families, and "creative" divorce.

For more than two decades, I have taught counseling theories courses and supervised counselors in their practices. In addition, I have carefully studied the methods and techniques used by marriage and family counselors. They developed their methods with the supporting premise that marriage and the family is a system which breaks down with improper use. The fashionable procedure is to fix damages that have occurred to this system. Counselors make repairs by coordinating the lives of family members in an orderly way that benefits everyone. They counsel or, more explicitly, "teach" husbands and wives the best methods and techniques for *getting along with each other*. They believe that together, in harmony, couples are then better able to manage their family systems.

Practitioners have developed this type of counseling to satisfy the mandate of the culture of our time - a culture of selfishness, ushered in by a generation of people whose center of life is in themselves. In their earlier developmental years, this generation of young people routinely used relationships for self-indulgence. Now, years later, having made the trek to the altar, as husbands and wives they fully expect to continue self-centered relating in their marriages.

Seriously disrupted relationships inevitably beset the marriages of this generation. One theorist after another has emerged with a behavioral counseling model to deal with these troubled marriages. They intentionally designed their models to directly teach husbands and wives how to refine their selfish behaviors, not to eliminate them. Although still self-centered, the refinement enables them to relate compatibly. The goal of their "counseling" is simply to make marriages work by controlling behavioral interactions. Regenerating love in the relationship and in the home is a secondary outcome, if it occurs at all.

We expect more in a home than a setting for meeting our physical needs. We want it to be a haven of love in which we constantly replenish our emotional and spiritual resources. Home should provide an escape from the grasp of a self-serving and uncaring world which takes from us what it needs and gives to us no more than its greed allows. At home I lay down my defensive armor, secure in the love that surrounds me. I am free to be me. I am open and trusting, completely vulnerable to personal and emotional injury, knowing that my loved ones will not take advantage of my vulnerability.

Psychotherapy is defined as "healing the mind." When we are tense, "stressed out," or torn by conflict, a professional "healer," using one or several therapeutic cures, helps us overcome our inner turmoil. In the same way, when a married couple, bonded in love, feels tension in its relationship, a *love relationship therapist* is needed, not a marriage counselor. Trained under today's standards of educational preparation, marriage counselors are not professionally qualified to heal broken loves. But they are competent to help couples revive failing marriages and family members to solve problems, resolve conflicts, reconcile differences, express feelings, reduce hostilities, clarify perceptions, and change behaviors. But they cannot help rebuild relationships on the foundation of love.

Families can peacefully co-exist without love by developing patterns of interactions that respect each other's rights. But when family members love each other, they have far more than just harmony in their relationships. They have the personal and emotional security of being comfortably nestled in the selfless devotion of trusted loved ones.

The type of therapy presented here does more than put a retread on a tired and worn-out marriage or family. *Love relationship therapy* has little in common with marriage counseling. A therapist, using the love model, helps couples build a bond of love which brings personal, physical, emotional, and spiritual enrichment to their lives. "Fixing" a marriage does not necessarily bind a husband and wife in love. But binding a couple in love does assure a successful marriage and a happier family.

Couples have trouble forming love-bonds because they do not understand the nature of love or the conditions under which it is expressed. Neither the counselor nor his clients know how to use it as a functional tool. Or more simply, they do not know how to move from *words* of love to *works* of love. The statement, "I love you," is an empty affirmation without active demonstrations of that love.

Not knowing how love works, clients and their counselors make the fundamental mistake of trying to rebuild a relationship on love, using it as a single unit of sentiment or thought. This doesn't work, because love is a complex network of interacting parts. Each part performs its work at different times and in different circumstances in the relationship.

From years of studying and practicing therapy, I have uncovered and clearly defined eight major components of love. These love components were notable, most often by their absence, in all of my marital cases. In eight of the final chapters I provide a detailed treatment of each of love's parts that compose the *whole* of love. I list them here in a capsule summary to introduce the reader to their form and substance. LOVE: 1) loves the source of love - the self made lovely by the in-dwelling God of love; 2) makes the pursuit of love a lifelong quest; 3) gives itself with no demand for love in return; 4) is an active servant; 5) allows the beloved to be different; 6) tries to experience the depth of the beloved's being so as to understand; 7) extends itself to meet the demands placed upon it; and 8) is always *mindful* of the loveliness of the one who has laid claim to it.

When I was a teenager growing up in a small rural community in Western Pennsylvania, boys from the "upper end" of town and boys from the "lower end" played a weekly baseball game. There were times when one of the teams came to play with only eight boys. But the game went on as scheduled. The team with eight players used only two outfielders. One was positioned in right field and the other in left. Each "shaded"-towards center field. This strategy reduced the size of the unprotected area in the middle of the outfield. But it also left larger positions of right and left fields with an inadequate defense. This strategy worked well until a ball was hit into one of the large undefended gaps created by this positioning of players. The ball could not be cut-off by either fielder. The batter usually got an extra base hit, a double or a triple, and frequently a home run. It couldn't be prevented because an action was required in the area of the field where there was no player to act.

I see this phenomenon at work in every troubled relationship in which I am invited to intervene. One or more of love's "team members" is absent from the spouses' interactions. My role as a therapist is to help them identify the member(s) not included in their relationship. Frequently, we find that the team member is present but performing poorly. The love-bond remains defective until the missing member is added to the team or the impaired member is restored to its full performing capacity.

Nearly all of the couples I work with profess love for one another. In our sessions we search for the love component that is either missing or failing, thereby preventing the relationship from deepening and growing. They learn that love is a team of interacting and interdependent players, and they learn how to use them as needed to keep the love-bond secured.

The love-bond is complete when both husband and wife field a total team of love. With teams at full strength, each responds with the appropriate part of love to any behavior shown by the other. The relationship cannot then become the casualty of a hateful conflict. Loving behaviors coming from this type of love-bonding are considerably different from the kind of love that we are accustomed to sharing. The style of loving which most of us practice and romanticize is tainted by our own needs. We expect to either benefit mutually from the exchange of our loves, or to be appreciated when we give love. I call it "physical love," not because it is sexual, but because it requires the physical senses to give and receive. When we embrace and kiss, we feel and taste it. When we say, "I love you," we hear it. When we receive a gift of love, we see it. And when one wears perfume or cologne, we smell the beauty of our beloved.

Some argue that love is not enough, that something more is needed to assure happiness and harmony in marriage.[1] And I agree, if they define love as the sharing of physical sensations, words, material gifts, and a pleasant fragrance. This love is not enduring. Physical sensations lose their stirring effect when touch is withdrawn. Words of love are canceled by careless neglect. Gifts of love lose their usefulness, or become worn with use, and no longer remind us of the love from which they came. And the scent of perfumes fades, becoming lost among all other smells. This physical love is too fragile to bind two people in a relationship that we expect to be strong enough to carry the burdens we place on it.

The love I speak of is much more able. It is spiritual and comes only with the *gift of oneself.* When I receive this love, the spirit of my being is touched by the spiritual presence of my beloved who gives it to me. It dries my tears, listens to my heartaches, stills my fears, grieves with me, encourages me during hardship, knows my unspoken hurts and soothes me, rejoices in my good fortunes, and shares in my merriment. Because it makes me first in her life, I need not compete with her self-love.

Truly this is a love that springs from the very Being of God, who is Love.[2] With His love in me, I see the loveliness of others even as He sees it. And I certainly see it in my wife whom I have taken into the intimacy of my heart and mind. I know it, trust it, and I open myself to receive it. Even as I receive it, I give it. We become one in spirit, united by a bond that if severed takes something from our beings. This love allows our individuality, but it won't permit us to be personally, emotionally, and spiritually estranged from one another.

Thousands of books and millions of words have been written about love. Theologians and biblical scholars are among those who have contributed to our understanding of love. When I was a theology student, I, too, enjoyed the study of the meaning of words in their original language - Greek and Hebrew. And, like many seminarians, I found the theological study of the "doctrine of love" to be most interesting.

Has anything new come out of these semantic investigations of the different words that have been used to express love? Not really. They have shown only how different people use love in different relationships. So we have universal love for humankind, friendship love for those with whom we feel close, passionate love for our spouses, compassionate love for family members, and courting love that brings a man and woman into a covenant. I won't bother to take you through an explanation of the Greek and Hebrew words from which each of these "loves" have been translated. You can read about them in any one of the hundreds of books written by religious writers who have made exegetical studies of this topic.

There is one love, and the source of that love is God. Love is the image of God stamped into every person. God is alive, therefore, in the world only when we give life to His love in us.

There is no such thing as "human love," only "divine love" expressed by humans. As such, it is spiritual, and we see it only when we show it in our relationships with others.

We know this love by its works. It has esteem for, and it highly values anyone to whom it is given. It always makes better not worse, builds up never tears down, and makes stronger not weaker. This love is committed to the good fortune of those it embraces. It personally, emotionally, and, most of all, spiritually lifts up those who are favored enough to receive it.

Whether in greater or lesser amounts, when we receive or give these blessings, it is that measure of divine love released through human voice and human touch. I invite you to join me on the following pages to learn how to breathe life into the spirit of this love that lies within you.

PART 1

The Breakup of
Love and Marriage

Millions of men and women live together outside of marriage. They belittle marriage saying, "It's only a piece of paper." These couples feel marriage does little more than provide social and government records, legitimize the birth of children, and serve as a moral sanction for sexual relations. Believing in their "progressive" cohabitation lifestyle, they discard marriage as a declining tradition.

Webster defines marriage as, "The institution whereby men and women are joined in a special kind of social and legal dependence for the purpose of founding and maintaining a family." Because a family can be "founded and maintained" by any man and woman at any time, these individuals, with their "advanced understanding," claim that marriage is a useless appendage. They ask, "We are in love, therefore, why should society or the law disallow our union?" The answer they expect, of course, is that they shouldn't. And so, a cohabiting man and woman insist on all the rights and privileges accorded to married couples and their families.

The Breakup of Love and Marriage

Marriage for these men and women is no longer revered. It requires a commitment they are reluctant to make. Marriage's legal binding takes away their freedom to end their relationships if love wanes and attraction for one another ebbs.

The elevation of the two individuals in the relationship has replaced the marriage institution that only their combined commitments can build. A man and woman, each pledged to self in a partnership of convenience, do not have the devotion of a husband and wife who forego their own needs and wishes for the good of a larger unit - home and family.

Consequently, this "progressive" change has produced a cultural shock. Social and moral ills are epidemic. And, ignoring their causes, citizens demand more laws and stricter enforcement, and more government intervention and infusion of money for programs and services to cure them. Rather than look for a prevention - stable homes and families managed by men and women bound in marriage by loving commitments - they allow the disease to run its course unabated.

In the first two chapters I explore the etiology of this change and the tottering state of the family, left in the wake of its unchecked rampage.

CHAPTER ONE

Love and Marriage

i love you. will you marry me?

In 1956, one of the top tunes on the popularity charts included the line, "Love and marriage go together like a horse and carriage ...you can't have one without the other." Young people listened, believing that love and marriage really did combine to unite a man and a woman in the most intimate personal, emotional, and physical relationship.

This was the traditional understanding of love and marriage: when two people are in love, ultimately they marry. And, if they married, it was assumed they were in love. With the exception of a marriage expediently arranged because of an unplanned pregnancy, love brought marriage into being, sustained it when a partner's initial commitment temporarily weakened, and protected it from all influences that subvert it. Love preceded marriage, and marriage, in turn, bound the relationship so that love could deepen and grow stronger.

But as time goes on, people change and so do traditions. Now, three decades later, with radically altered social institutions, we need to re-examine our understanding of love and marriage. Many people end up in loveless marriages. Many others live together in love without marriage.[1]

Love and Marriage

In my professional practice, I have learned to distinguish between a marriage-bond and a love-bond. I no longer assume that love is the "tie that binds" couples in their marital relationships. And I cannot always rely on the presence of love to lead them through a friendly disentanglement from the vengeful anger that ensnares their feelings when interpersonal clashes disrupt the harmony in their relationship.

Increasingly, marriage counselors are asked to help couples, *who lack a bond of love,* to restore stability to their troubled marriages. So, when they try to use the strength of love to help couples achieve understanding and compatibility, they reach an impasse. They discover early in treatment a relationship built on a weak foundation - a marriage certificate and a formal pronouncement, "I now declare you to be husband and wife." By introducing love, counselors only confuse the issues.

Sadly, over the last 30 years we have seen how easily this foundation crumbles. Courts nullify marriage certificates with divorce documents. A judge says, "You are *no longer* husband and wife." Couples burdened with stress and tension welcome dissolution of the marriage contract as an easily attainable source of relief. Marriage unites two people, but in our "liberated" society it can't hold them together.

Husbands and wives who don't distinguish between love and marriage try to resolve their conflicts by using marriage as the reason why each "should," "ought," or "must" behave as the other demands. When I press a wife or husband about why he or she expects a particular behavior, I receive answers such as, "She is just as obligated as I am," or "It's only fair that he does the same as I am willing to do," or "Why should I care about it anymore than she does?"

They believe the ceremonial union in marriage is accompanied by self-regulating behaviors that control the relationship.

Further, they endow marriage with the power to enforce those behaviors. Why should they be responsible, obligated, fair, and caring? Whether stated or implied, their answer is, "After all, we're married."

Married couples, and their marriage counselors, seldom consider that the devotion husbands and wives expect from one another is the fruit of love, not the product of marriage. Marriage is a contractual arrangement and provides to the contracting parties only the benefits contained within it.[2] Yet, when I help a couple in a marital dispute to restore harmony in their relationship, I often find they want more than the contract can give.

While browsing for a wedding card to send to a young couple, I came upon a message that clearly confuses the meanings of love and marriage.

MARRIAGE JOINS TWO PEOPLE IN THE CIRCLE OF ITS LOVE

Marriage deepens and enriches every facet of life. Happiness is fuller . . . memories are fresher; commitment is stronger . . . Marriage understands and forgives the mistakes life is unable to avoid. It encourages and nurtures new life, new experiences . . .
-Edmund O'Neill[3]

The heading to this prosaic verse implies that love is intrinsic to marriage. Yet, marriage has love only when the two people who have been united by it love each other. Unfortunately, many people who believe the erroneous message, marry hoping to find love. But love is present in marriage only when it is in the hearts and minds of a man and woman who marry. So, it's better to say, "Love Joins Two People In the Circle of Marriage."

The author then went on to attribute to marriage other functions that it doesn't have. "Marriage deepens and enriches every facet of life." Because of marriage, "Happiness is fuller, memories are fresher, commitment is stronger ...Marriage understands and forgives the mistakes life is unable to avoid. It encourages and nurtures new life, new experiences..."

When husbands and wives do not receive these gifts from their marriage, they become disillusioned and call a marriage counselor. In counseling they accuse each other of failing to provide what they believe was promised - a deep and enriched life, full happiness, fresh memories, strong commitment, understanding, forgiveness, encouragement, and nurture. Most marriage counselors try to help them obtain these blessings while ignoring their source. They come only from the bounties of love, not from marriage agreements.

The distinctive features of the marriage contract limit its capacity to fulfill the personal and emotional needs of a husband and wife. Contracts are used by two people, or groups of people, to define their relationship and to specify the behaviors expected from each other. Contracts are drawn because we do not trust each other to honor principles upon which our relationship has been established. Whereas contracts harbor distrust, the act of loving expresses total confidence that one will receive as much or more than is given. Love doesn't require a bludgeon to be held over one's head as a constant reminder that the outcome of a broken commitment will be a grievous penalty. Love oversees itself. It propels itself toward a harvest of kindness, tenderness, and goodwill.

When two parties bargain toward an agreement, each hopes to give little and to receive much. It is understood that issues will be argued from an egocentric reference, that is, each will be guided by his or her own best interest. They make it clear that my needs, not your needs, determine what I will or won't accept.

When a couple enters therapy, each party blames the other for failing to give what they feel the marital contract stipulates. They rarely confess their own unfulfilled responsibilities in the marriage. They view the breakdown with the same self interest that prompted them to marry.

Couples in marriage counseling use the marriage-bond as the platform from which they discuss divisive issues. Under-pinning this platform are obligation, responsibility, and duty. The injured spouse uses these binding powers to demand that the violating party honor contractual commitments. One who feels wrongfully treated pleads his or her case from a position of entitlement. The unspoken reasoning is, "I have a right to the benefits in our marriage agreement."

In this instance, the counselor helps the parties renegotiate, to mediate a settlement, and to restore harmony to their marriage. As an objective participant in the negotiating process, the counselor identifies and clarifies the areas in which one or both have violated their agreement. Marriage counselors are more comfortable functioning as conciliators than as therapists. In this latter role they would help their clients heal injured feelings and broken spirits, not simply arbitrate differences.

When I supervise marriage counseling trainees in a family services agency, I receive copies of the intake records of couples before counseling begins. The intake counselor collects the information, makes preliminary diagnoses, and recommends treatment. On one such record, the counselor had written that the husband, married for 19 years, had lost all feelings of love for his wife. Noting that the emotional distance within the couple had widened, the husband stated, "Either put the relationship back together or separate." He went on to say that he was considering ending the marriage.

In his case conceptualization, the intake counselor suggested that the "...renegotiation of the marital contract, communication, and conflict management should receive primary attention." Secondarily, the treatment counselor was advised to focus on individual issues such as the husband's "inability to be emotionally available" and the wife's "...depression and low self-esteem."

The intake counselor had overlooked the crucial issue in this deteriorating marriage. The relationship, according to the husband, was breaking up because he could no longer feel love for his wife. Lacking the nurture of warm and affectionate caring, the relationship and the marriage were unable to thrive.

Despite the husband's admission that he might leave the relationship, the intake counselor recommended that the couple negotiate a new marriage agreement. The new contract would include the husband's intention to be emotionally available to his wife. I asked, "Without the prompting of love, how could this objective be achieved? Could the husband relate emotionally as a matter of contractual obligation?" If so, this is nothing more than the counselor's reminder to the husband that he has failed in his *marriage duty*. But why, given his reluctance to be a marriage partner, would the husband agree to be forced into complying with this article in the contract? He would not. More likely, he would dissolve the marriage through divorce and accept the penalties incurred for breaking the contract.

How different is a relationship when devoted love is the bond that unites a man and a woman. When loveliness in one arouses love in another, no contract is needed to enforce fidelity. Love is non-negotiable. To love is an honor, not an obligation. Love does not bargain to give itself only when it receives equally. Because love wants only the privilege of giving, it doesn't experience the pressure of duty or the irritation of responsibility. Love always entreats, "Please accept the warmth of my devotions." And when accepted, it never fails to commit totally. Conversely, one who loves is deeply saddened when told, "Your love is not needed or wanted."

In the ritual, marriage is called "holy and honorable," and is described as the "most beautiful of all relationships." But, marriage cannot attain such loftiness without the love of two people who shape it into these images.

Love is empowered inwardly to move toward another. Because the loveliness of another person awakens the ardor of its affection, love doesn't require external compulsions to cause it to act. The marital contract uses the sovereignty of law to force two persons to remain in marriage or to free them from it. Love binds two people in a relationship and uses marriage to solemnize and sanctify it.

As a marriage counselor supervisor for more than 13 years, I have observed that counselors rarely distinguish between the marriage-bond and the bond of devoted love. They may ask each marriage partner, "Do you love your husband? wife?" And even when the responses convey serious doubt, or are honest admissions that love has withered and died, these counselors proceed as though it's fully present. They attempt to help couples resolve personal conflicts, to heal emotional hurts, to remove obstacles related to value differences, and to restore faithfulness to broken commitments because they are, after all, united in marriage.

But these changes which marriage counselors hope to bring about are really the fruits of devoted loving. As I stated earlier, the marriage-bond is little more than a social and legal contract that does not have the strength to bear the strains that occur within intimate relationships. Only the deep and enduring love of two people in marriage can hold the relationship together when conflicts occur.

Professionally and ethically, I believe counselors should explain to their clients how methods employed for resolving troubling issues differ from those used in a love-bonded relationship. When a husband and wife are not in love, they negotiate their differences from the "I" and the "me" positions. In this type of counseling, the counselor uses the personal and emotional qualities of tenderness, warmth and sensitivity sparingly as they work to achieve marital harmony.

When there is no bond of devoted love, a counselor deals largely with justice and fairness, concessions and compromises, management and reorganization, contracts and stipulations, and responsibilities and obligations. In trying to help couples resolve their differences and restore harmony, the counselor facilitates, arbitrates, and negotiates, but focuses little on love.

In this capacity, a marriage counselor becomes a technician who specializes in the behavioral correction of broken marriages. Essentially, this technician is expected to identify the areas in the marriage in which the two parties have failed to behave according to the marriage agreement. Serving as professional specialists, marriage "technicians" help their clients to understand the conditions in the covenant that they have breached, and then urge them to revert to those behaviors that comply with marriage guidelines. As an expert in facilitation and mediation, the technician guides them into accepting all that marriage stipulates and implies.

If, however, a husband and wife are in love, they will have given each other the central position in their lives. When these couples tell me that they have problems, I do not think of them as troubled marriages. I conceptualize and treat them as broken love relationships in need of repair.

I label myself a "love relationship therapist," not "marriage counselor." In this role I help them restore their relationship by exploring how the love they have declared for each other is not reflected in loving practice. I use interpretations and clarifications as therapeutic tools to assist them in achieving these insights. Together we analyze specific problems in terms of a weakness in their bond of loving devotion. We focus upon the nature of love at work, not the selfish interests and demands of two individuals lamenting their unhappiness and frustration.

When one spouse loves and the other doesn't, the task of a love relationship therapist is more difficult. The one who loves insists upon the considerations that love normally demonstrates. The one who doesn't love provides only the considerations that selfishness permits and the marriage requires.

How does a therapist conceptualize and treat such a troubled relationship? What goals can be reasonably established? How does a therapist handle a relationship in which one has been accustomed to giving and the other taking? Can a therapist, by defining the relationship and clarifying misunderstandings and assumptions, help them rekindle mutual love? Indeed, can a relationship be maintained when one is marriage-bonded and the other is love-bonded?

Todd and Cora

Often I work with husbands and wives, both of whom acknowledge the legally-binding status of their marriage, although only one avows a deep and enduring love for the other. Cora, a self-employed businesswoman, came to me for help to untangle her confused feelings for her husband, Todd. She married Todd when she was eighteen years old and the mother of a three-year-old child. Following the marriage, Cora and her husband moved into a house owned by his parents, located a short distance from their home. Todd and his father operated a family automotive repair business. He worked six days a week, often twelve hours a day. Dutifully, Cora took on the role of a wife: cooking, cleaning, washing, canning during the summer months, and caring for the lawn and garden.

Largely to please Todd, the couple had three children of their own. Cora became the primary parent, responsible for the care of the three children. Yet, she found time to attend real estate classes. Eventually, with her license, she established a full-time real estate sales practice. For twenty years she combined the roles of faithful wife, devoted mother, dedicated homemaker, and tireless business operator.

At age thirty-eight, Cora turned inward to her feelings, locked in silence by the pressure of daily demands and by her conscientious attention to the roles and tasks which family members expressly or implicitly assigned to her. She grew bitter and angry, feeling the family had selfishly used her services but had not appreciated the love and devotion from which they flowed.

Cora held Todd responsible for their marriage's failure to be as fulfilling for her as it was for him. Cora told Todd that she felt she no longer loved him, and she suggested that they separate until she could come to terms with her feelings. Todd was shattered. In therapy he was unable to hold back his tears and repeatedly stated that he loved her and did not know how he could live without her. Ignoring Todd's effort to change her mind, and unaffected by his loving entreaties, Cora moved out of the house.

During the therapy sessions that followed, Cora spoke in great detail about the injustices she felt she had endured as a wife, mother, and homemaker. Given the opportunity to express and, at times, emotionally re-experience what had happened, she gradually set herself free from the control of her blind sense of moral rightness which she used to justify her withdrawal from the home. With the veil of her emotional pain and vengeful anger removed, Cora's perception of the home in general, and her husband in particular, changed. She no longer viewed Todd's character as offensive as she did before. She saw a more pleasant man to whom she was attracted.[4] With newly discovered feelings for Todd and the ebbing of her resentment and anger, Cora wanted to rejoin the family. She anticipated sharing in a love relationship, rather than just being bound in wedlock.

When Cora told Todd of her decision to return, she was unprepared for his reaction. Just four months earlier Todd asserted that he loved Cora and that he would be deeply grieved if she moved from the home. Now, he said that he was confused and needed time to determine if he still loved her. Although she yearned to rejoin the family, Cora accurately reasoned that the relationship with Todd, following her return, would be no different from when she left. It would be she, however, who would be bonded in love to her spouse. He, in turn, would simply submit to the relationship as a duty in the marriage covenant.

If Todd can sort through his confusion and gain some insights into their relationship's true character, he may be able to turn his mind from himself to his wife and to search for her loveliness. If, however, he allows himself to remain emotionally confused, persuaded that he is a victim of his wife's betrayal, he will not discover the beauty she harbors within. A mutual love bond will not develop and flourish.

If they choose to live together with their conflict unresolved, Cora will seek ways to practice the love she holds for her husband. He, however, will perform his roles as a grudging marriage obligation, without fervor or romance. She will crave more personal and emotional intimacy; he will devise more ways to avoid closeness. She will be disappointed and saddened because her attempts to secure love will have widened their emotional distance. He will be sullen and angered, unable to elude the demands to gratify her longings. They will have exchanged positions within the relationship. He will now be in a marriage only; she will be in a marriage and in love. And the therapist will be back in the same challenging role, trying to help them find personal happiness and emotional fulfillment from a relationship in which one is bonded with love and the other with marriage.

*   *   *

Love and marriage do go together, but they also can and do exist separately. In a marriage in which only one spouse loves, difficult choices have to be made when the spouse who has been giving the love demands that love be mutually binding. Should a wife who has for many years loved unselfishly, but received only token love from her husband, continue to be loving?

One distraught wife, in tears, presented this dilemma to me, hoping for a solution in which her husband would become a "lover" in their marriage. After we had processed her heartaches and feelings of despair, I attempted to touch upon some of the personal attributes and psychological dynamics that seemed to account for her husband's attitudes. Interrupting me, she asked, "Why are we discussing my husband when I am the one who is hurting?"

To show the relationship between her feelings and her husband's emotional emptiness, I offered this illustration. If someone repeatedly lowers a pail into a well for water to quench a thirst, and each time the pail is returned empty, it does no good to curse the empty well. When she understood that for 27 years she had been seeking relief from her emotional thirst by returning again and again to a husband who had no love to give, she realized the fault lay not in his failure but in her senseless expectations. She began to understand that she had been on an endless quest to secure love from someone in whom it did not exist.

Early in her marriage she formed a message which she played over and over in her mind, "I need love. You are my husband. You are required to give me the love I need." Turning off the message, she began to explore her new options. Should she continue giving love, simply to preserve the marriage and go on enduring her painful emotional emptiness? Could she develop supporting emotional relationships with female friends in similar dilemmas, and remain in her marriage sustained by its benefits? Should she dissolve the marriage and find a relationship with another man who would love her in the same measure she would love him? Should she delay a decision, hoping to persuade her husband to join her in therapy to deal with their love issues, assisting him to discover her loveliness, and to learn the art of loving? The last option will successfully reunite them only if both are willing to develop and nurture a bond of devoted love.

Love and Marriage

Love has become a worn-out word. It continues to be a sentimental theme for romantics who write songs and plots for novels and stage plays. But marital counselors, as well as the millions of men and women entering marriage, use it less frequently as the bond for securing relationships.

If therapists and their patients choose a *love treatment approach*, they must understand the full magnitude of its *self-lessness* and the depth to which it reaches. Love can't help reconcile differences between two individuals in a relationship if it is not permitted the complete range of its power and influence. Behaviors and communications must be subjected to its scrutiny to determine if they are expressions of true love.

Love relationship therapy may, for the first time, show a husband and wife the true meaning of love. Therapists who use it, quickly discover that their teaching function is as important to the restoration of harmony as is the exercise of their professional therapeutic skills. The treatise on love in the latter portion of this book gives marital therapists and troubled marriage partners a fuller understanding of how "love in action" heals divisions and binds two lives into one.

CHAPTER TWO

Love, Marriage and the Family System

"an impossible dream,"
a happy marriage and family without the sweetness of love

Marriage and the family are struggling to weather the changes that have removed them from their long-held position of honor in American society. Nearly one of every two marriages ends in divorce. And the concept of "family" is now so confusing that it needs to be explained before it can be understood. Within its definitions are the "split family," the "single parent family," the "blended family," and the "intact family." The concept of parent is even less precise. Rearing a child may be the custodial parent, the court appointed parent, the adoptive parent, the foster parent, or the biological parent. Finally, we can never be quite certain about the child's relationship to the parents. If the youngster is not the natural child of both parents, it may be a foster child, an adopted child, a stepchild, the father's child, or the mother's child. As many as one-half of all homes are composed of individuals from diverse backgrounds and experiences. They come together to form a "family" in which each member hopes to find a happy life.

Love, Marriage and the Family System

Why has this dismantling of the American family taken place? Although it is not within the scope of this book to discuss the disintegration of civilization's most steadfast social system, the family, there are some explanations for its collapse that I find amusing. The February 1988 issue of *Psychology Today* contains several such explanations. Robert J. Trotter in his short essay, "To Have And To Hold - Four Years,"[1] quotes Helen Fisher, an anthropologist with the American Museum of Natural History, who states that divorce takes place at one of three peaks in marriage. Further, she believes that these peaks are determined possibly by "brain physiology" rather than by societal forces. The peaks occur "...among couples married for four years, among people between the ages of 25 and 29, and among those with no children or one dependent child."

In another article, "Married with Child,"[2] Judy Berlfein relates that Ann Crouter, associate professor of Human Development at the Pennsylvania State University, and her colleagues found that husbands whose wives are employed spend more time with their children than husbands who are sole supporters of the family. However, greater involvement with the children was accompanied by greater unhappiness with the marriage. The authors concluded that there is insufficient time and energy for husbands and wives to be together to bind their relationship. They also opined that some men may resent the increased responsibility for household tasks.

A third article, by Christopher Joyce, "These Machines Want To Help You,"[3] relates that Elaine Bleckman, a clinical psychologist at Albert Einstein College of Medicine - Montefiore Medical Center, feels family and spousal conflicts are due to communication failures and to the lack of "straightforward negotiation" skills. And she contends that computer games can be used to correct these communicative deficiencies.

18

Also, in this issue of *Psychological Today,* psychologist Paul Chance writes that "The Trouble [is] With Love."[4] He perceives romantic love as a "menace" and feels the world will be a "...sane and more sensible place when lovesickness has been eradicated." With the absence of this love, people will be more "cool-headed" and "rational about their mates." Presumably they also will be more inclined to remain together and be happy in their marriages. In support of his thesis, Chance quotes Joseph Wolpe, an eminent behavioral psychologist, who says that love is a "bad habit." It is an "emotional habit" that is "resistant to logical arguments or good advice." Wolpe says love cannot be found in the cortex-thinking part of the brain. It is located in the "...deeper more reptilian brain - the same part of the brain that makes the shark go into a feeding frenzy." In addition, Chance cites psychologist Lawrence Casler who says "love is a cultural invention" which people use to engage in guilt-free sex." Love's only purpose is to make sex morally right.

Finally, S. Phillip Morgan, a University of Pennsylvania researcher quoted in *Behavior Today,* found that married couples are less likely to divorce if the child in the family is a male.[5] Presumably, the father is more likely to remain in the family to parent and to relate to the male child with whom he can experience a more intimate identity.

Even if all of these factors play some role in the decline of the family, how do we use them to prevent its continuing deterioration? Actually, such information helps little to restore the family's influence in shaping the lives within its circle. These researchers haven't taken seriously the loss of the family's eminence. Sincere attempts to explore reasons for the family's declining importance must focus on more substantive research than is found in the literature. To attribute the failure of mar-

19

riage to "brain physiology," for example, is little more than a calloused, biting attack on marriage and the family. Scoffing at the family's present plight appeals to some, but it doesn't contribute to the recovery of the family's importance.

Probably nothing is more far-reaching in the life of an individual than family membership. The family is expected to provide in some measure for all the needs of its members. Today, in its disarray, the family is not equal to this task.

Can individuals from varied backgrounds and experiences, at different ages and stages of growth, be assembled into a functional unit in which the prosperity of all is the foremost concern of each? Without the natural bond between members, can there be a family tie? As an adopted family member, is an individual loyal primarily to first attachments and only secondarily to new relationships? Can the family in which both parents are present, and all children born from their union, survive the assaults from our society to undermine and prevent it from fulfilling the mission historically charged to it?

Prior to World War II, the American family was a venerated social unit, strong enough to endure any storm. In the years that followed, relentless assaults have left the family in a tottering state. The hard questions are these: Will the traditional family become a vestige of the past? Will it be abandoned to make way for the "modern family" with its claim to provide a greater potential for all of its members?

We can't answer these questions without understanding the extent to which the family has been uprooted and fundamentally changed over the last thirty years. The blending of several family members into a single unit has been replaced by a system in which *each member wants to function as the unit*. As such, individual welfare supersedes collective good. Intimacy and personal care for one another yield to emotional distancing and self-seeking. The home is no longer a respite to which family members retreat when life's burdens become too heavy, and all energy and the will to persist have been depleted.

The role of the family as a molder of values has been turned over to the school or the church, or to any other group willing to help persons who are seeking acceptance and belonging. And because the values that enter the home from many different sources conflict with one another, intra-family clashes are unavoidable.

Family members have come to expect from the home only the satisfaction of physical needs - food, shelter, safety. They go outside of the home to be personally understood, to find emotional intimacy, and to pursue happiness. Because they derive so much of life's meaning from their careers, social activities, and personal relationships unimportant to the home, they take little responsibility for family unity.

Perhaps these changes were inevitable and necessary, but the quickness with which they came has created a void. There is no adequate substitute to perform the roles the family has relinquished.

Rushing in to fill this void is the typical marriage and family counselor who believes problems and conflicts reflect the failure of the "family system" rather than the egocentricity of the family members. Theoretically, in their view, the system is functioning properly only when the individuals in it have learned to form personal interlacements in which the needs of each are met. So, when problems surface, it is the system that is broken and needs repair. When the system works well, it ensures the happiness and prosperity of all its members. This is analogous to faulty machinery producing a defective product. The operator can either correct the defect in each piece after it is produced or repair the machine so that it creates a flawless product.

Love, Marriage and the Family System

In the last 20 years family systems counseling has become an elaborate and complex specialty within an expanded range of human services. It is applied routinely as the treatment of choice by most marriage counselors. Central to the systemic approach is the skill and influence of the family counselor.

The counselor must be a systems expert who understands how each member relates as an integral component in the orderly performance of total family functioning. The counselor performs many roles. He or she is the *family ombudsman* who patiently listens to the complaints of unhappy members and empathically shares the feelings of those who are emotionally distressed. When the change process begins, the counselor determines the issues upon which a member or the entire family should *focus*. The basic intervention techniques the counselor uses are the *reframing* of perceptions and the *coaching* of members on the behaviors that should reasonably spring from those perceptions. Often the counselor assumes a position of *proximity* with a family member or becomes part of a *coalition* of one or more members to facilitate understanding, or to expedite the change process. As an arbiter, the counselor *negotiates boundaries* to protect the rights and privacies of those members who have neither the courage nor the skills to fend for themselves. *Crisis induction* is frequently used to secure diagnostic data or to force the adoption of more appropriate behaviors. As a skillful manager of the development of new family interactions and behaviors, the counselor *mediates* disagreements, *instructs* members seeking specific directions, *mentors* those who need a model to emulate, and *sometimes does personal counseling*. In all of these ways, the counselor *restructures* the family to produce a well-functioning unit. Successful treatment of the system depends upon the ability of the counselor to break through the *homeostatic rigidity* which controls the family's maladaptive styles of relating. Although the counselor is the central figure in the systemic approach, he or she must avoid *over-centralization,* i.e., shifting the attention from the process to himself and his role.

Concurrent with the "counseling," the family undergoes a continuing and penetrating analysis. Serving as a system's analyst, the counselor directly examines the relationships and interactions of all members in the family unit. Since neither the diagnosis nor the treatment can be planned in advance, the family is observed and studied in its setting. Dispassionately, the counselor identifies the problems that are inhibiting successful family interactions. Data are gathered by *tracking* the *transactional patterns* of the family members and by looking for evidence of *scape goating* or the *detouring* of conflicts and feelings through an innocent parent or child. The counselor is alert to the presence of *triads, subsystems,* and *enmeshments,* as well as to *systems maintenance* behaviors that are repressing *individualization* of any family member. It is often necessary to construct a *genogram* to ascertain the extent to which there is a residual effect from unresolved conflicts originating in the family of origin that has carried over into the present family. In like manner, the exploration of *genetic endowment* frequently yields information that helps explain behaviors and interactions. Essentially, then, the counselor is a trouble-shooter called in by the family to locate the areas of distress and restore a peaceful flow of interactions among its members.

At this point you are probably saying to me, "Zimmerman, you have had me read a lot of technical terms that only confuse rather than enlighten me." And I reply, "You got my point." The counselor is bogged down in the use of a lot of cumbersome tools, that when properly used, "fix" the system. It doesn't matter that the parts, i.e., family members in this repaired system, must settle for harmony in relating without loving regard for one another.

If the reader is interested in learning more about the family systems approach to marital and family counseling, I refer you to the works of Salvadore Minuchin. You may find his works interesting, providing your mind is given to logical analysis and step-by-step problem resolution.[6]

This brief description of the systems approach to marriage and family counseling shows clearly that the counselor does not view the family as *kin united by love*. Instead, it is seen and treated as a microcosm of the larger society which advocates individualism. As such, family members put aside their individualism only when stubbornly clinging to it results in personal pain, or in a loss that is greater than its benefits.

Today, the egocentric lifestyle is fashionable and is promoted shamelessly in every segment of society. Beginning in the 1970s with the "me" generation, it is now the prime mover in the lives of the great majority of people. They associate with others for personal gain, not to move in harmony with them. And the family has fallen prey to this avarice. Members exalt themselves while, at the same time, refusing to commit to the well-being of the larger group in which they hold their trusted membership.

In major works written on family systems counseling there is no reference to "love" in either the tables of contents or in the general indexes. Clearly, this means that leaders in the development of the systems approach have structured family counseling to exclude love. It is neither a directing influence in the treatment process nor an outcome of the process.

24

Come Into My Life

Family counselors cannot be accused of deception. Obviously, they have given up on love. It is not included even as window dressing. Responsibility is substituted for love, and interpersonal harmony replaces personal caring.

Establishing new lines of accountability, working out more productive patterns of interaction, and implementing new guidelines for behavior are the major objectives of family counselors. The attitudes and feelings of the family members are expected to comply with these objectives. Solving problems and eliminating conflicts are achieved primarily by inhibiting the offenders' use of others for personal gain. No meaningful attempt is made to help them examine their unlovely behaviors, or to appreciate the loveliness of those whose lives are hurt by their transgressions.

By reducing the family to a system with only a limited role for emotions and feelings, the counselor hopes to produce a network of interacting people with minimal loss of self-centeredness. All family members are taught to identify their rights and the boundaries within which they can exercise those rights. They are free to live in the center of their own lives within these defined limits, to the extent to which they don't violate the rights of others in the family. The system is respected at all times, and all family members must adjust their demands to its productive capacities.

Surrendering to the seemingly invincible power of selfishness, the family counselor attempts to put it into a system in which it can be controlled. Individuals within the system reserve the right to pursue ego-dominated lives, but they cannot depreciate the quality of living of other family members.

No one may direct the energies of the total system to him/herself, nor is the system allowed to place the burden of its successful operation upon the shoulders of a single family member. Frequently, however, the latter is attempted by assigning a parent, usually the mother, as a *family switchboard operator.* She passes along messages between family members who are in conflict. If the conflict remains unresolved or, as often happens, becomes more intensified, she suffers the weariness of the struggle and bears the guilt of failure.

The counselor skillfully repairs the system so that daily it buzzes on while producing individually-satisfied egocentric drones. "Living," in this process, is replaced by "movement." The family counselor has de-emotionalized the home environment and changed human beings into automatons. They perform according to the bionic program created for them by their behavioral craftsman. It is no small wonder that the members of this joyless system seek relationships with life-spirited people outside of the home. Here they find persons with whom they can relate emotionally and can experience the feeling of being understood. These outside relationships are not entirely satisfying, but they do provide vitality and togetherness that otherwise are missing from their lives.

Defending their practice, family counselors say the family has become more complex, and requires a more elaborate system than simply "relating with love" to deal successfully with these complexities. But it is more accurate to say that the family is deteriorating because its members have regressed to a child-like level of self-indulgence. At this level, "I" overrules "we," "me" overshadows "us," and "my" precedes "ours."

Diverting attention from others to self is simple. The family becomes complex only when one or more of its members resort to manipulating others in order to be in the center of their living. Then, a counselor is called to enter into the complicated process of sorting out the patterns of scheming interactions and behaviors that self-indulging members use to subvert the system, or to take advantage of selected members of the system, for their own use.

Family life is not complicated necessarily by the blending of children from different parents or by the out-of-home employment of both parents. Many such families have demonstrated that with love they can develop and maintain just as happy and functional units as "traditional" families. Rather, problems result from the self-seeking behaviors of the individuals who, regardless of their past, comprise the family. The extent of conflict relates directly to the number of members who live only for themselves and greedily use any indulgence that is given, or that can be extracted from others in the family. Only in this sense has the family become more complex.

The image of the family system operating like a cybernetic machine, grinding away mindlessly as each interaction is entered, is depressing. Yet, it illustrates life in today's American household. A favor is done in exchange for a favor. Tasks are accepted as assigned responsibilities. Rules of conduct are obeyed to avoid punishment. Mothers and fathers provide for the needs of their children to avoid the label, "poor parents." Verbal or physical abuse against another is forbidden simply as a rule of conduct and intra-familial propriety. Activities are planned to accommodate "fairly and reasonably" the various desires of parents and children. The system turns out these kinds of behaviors as a practiced discipline. Members know that they receive copious benefits from the home that aren't available from any other person or group. Therefore, they hold the family together, requiring self-interests at times to be renounced. Self-indulgence is checked, when needed, in a trade for the advantages that come from affiliation with others in the family.

Members go through the act of relating, but the spirit of family is missing. And genuine feeling for one another is offered sparingly. Favors lack true warmth. Tasks done for another person are performed with little thoughtfulness. Personal gains replace benevolence as the reason for obeying rules of the home. Parenting is a moral charge lacking affection. Members may not behave abusively, but neither do they freely express kindness. Concessions are made without charity when planning family activities.

Without joy, family life is a dreary routine - a somber ritual lacking the glow of smiling faces. Relationships are listless interactions in which the involved members detach themselves from feelings. Expressions of sensitivity and emotion are limited primarily to outbursts of anger.

The systemic approach has developed logically in response to the swing of the social pendulum from "us" to "me." In this position people move impassively among themselves, emotionally unmoved by the adversities and troubled lives of others. They do not want to be burdened with the heavy feelings of persons beset by misfortune. In those instances when they do reach out to others in need, their assistance flows from a sense of moral obligation, rather than from a loving and caring heart. For their generosity, they receive only the satisfaction of a duty fulfilled. They cannot know the feelings of joy that come to people whose freely-given love heals the affliction of others.

Howard Means, a syndicated columnist commenting on the movie, "Throw Momma From The Train," provides a poignant statement about our loveless society. He writes, "As in almost every other movie these days, men and women in 'Throw Momma' make love without any love ...the highest emotion anyone seems capable of aspiring to is not much more than good old-fashioned lust for money, fame, someone else's body, whatever." This "lust" is rooted in a love that is centered in self.

Come Into My Life

The family is languishing because it is a microcosm of the loveless society that encircles it. Family members do not allow the good of others to replace the selfish demands which shape their attitudes and direct their behaviors. In their quest for self-indulgence they use persuasion, appeasement, or duplicity to reduce one another to a hireling. Love is active only in the elevation of self.

Love makes the difference. The 19th century political figure and diplomat, Charles Francis Adams, recorded in his diary, "Went fishing with my son today ...a day wasted." On the same day, his son, Brook Adams, who also kept a daily journal, made this entry, "Went fishing today with my father ...the most wonderful day of my life." The elder Adams viewed the activity and the relationship with his son as a parental task. He carried it out as an assignment. Although anxiously awaiting the end of tedium, he respectfully attended to his son.

But Brook, beaming with affection for his father, cheerfully entered into a loving relationship with him. Looking up at his father with glowing endearment, he rejoiced in each fleeting moment of togetherness.

Family life without love makes self-giving begrudging, while love in the family makes living an opportunity for enthusiastic giving. With love in our lives, deeds are never chores forced upon us. They are charitable actions eagerly taken in obedience to the entreaty of love. Love compels a husband or wife, a parent or child, a brother or sister to reach out to one another to ease life's distresses.

Love, alone, can empower the home to retain the allegiance of its members. Love flowing freely from and among them unites their spirits. It binds them in a mutual commitment to group living for the good of each and all. Love coming from significant others is readily trusted for "it does not seek its own?"[7] Love yields to the request for help because it has no being until it is breathed into action, and no value until it is given to another. Love does not allow an individual to pursue pleasures without determining how it affects others in the family. When love abounds, the family learns quickly that loving is living and living is loving. Interactions are no longer behaviors within the system, but expressions of love for the system. The system is promoted because its members generate love which, in turn, is channeled to those who need its life-nurturing care. A loving family member wants to know when another member needs its generous help, when the comforting effect of compassion can lift a broken spirit, when humor can change a frown to a smile, when the strength of forbearance may share a weighty burden, or when understanding could help solve a problem.

Is family counseling, with its emphasis on the "system," appropriate to treat a dysfunctional family? If the purpose is simply to reduce interpersonal conflicts, and promote functional relationships, the answer is a qualified "yes." Qualified, because conflicts often re-emerge and relationships break down when the discipline of self-restraint weakens. When the discipline cannot be controlled, the family counselor is called again to repair the system.

If the intent of a systems counselor is to restore functional unity and, at the same time, breathe an exhilarating spirit of closeness, caring, and collective loving into the family, the answer is an unqualified "no." The systems approach cannot do this because it lacks the unyielding power of love, which alone is strong enough to turn back even the most relentless demands of selfishness. Love can perform this role because its mission is to selflessly attend to the happiness and well-being of those who need its service.

PART II

A New Paradigm of Human Relationships

Relationships unite the human species in a common purpose - perpetuating itself. We all relate, but for many people this brings daily irritations. And, for others, relationships cause debilitating anxiety. In some instances they end in conflicts with verbal or physical attacks on one another. While we can't live without relating, we don't know how to relate in ways that enhance living.

Our problem is not in the interactions themselves, but in the motives that control them. Behaviors often conceal the real purposes that draw us into relationships. When trust in one another's integrity is betrayed by covert motives, relationship failures follow.

Blindly trusting in relationships in a culture that encourages individualism and self-promotion invites interpersonal conflict and personal disappointment. Wisdom tells us that it's foolish to always relate to others believing that they have our welfare in mind. Sometimes they do; usually they do not.

It isn't as difficult to determine peoples' motives as we may have believed. Relationships are generally clearly defined, if we look at them as they are, not as we wish them to be. In Chapter Three I present a relationship model that enables us to accurately interpret motives. Then, in Chapter Four, I provide a second dimension of the model that explains what happens when we enter blindly into relationships - when the "heart" overrules the "head."

CHAPTER THREE

Relationships
With Pure Bonding

the bond is the bridge we build from my life to yours

Life is relating, and relationships are the heartbeat of life. We relate in a variety of ways - with words, gestures, facial expressions, or actions. And the reasons for relating are just as varied. We share in relationships to inform, direct, persuade, control, or make exchanges. Relationships may be pleasant and anxiously anticipated, necessary but boring, formal and dull, or required but resented. One fact is certain, we do not live without relating.

We long for human contact. Imagine being the only person living in a country that had been heavily populated. Driving on a highway knowing that you will not meet or be overtaken by a fellow motorist, walking the streets of a city without brushing the shoulder of another pedestrian, turning on a television or a radio and seeing no human form and hearing no human voice, or speaking and having no one to hear and respond to you - these are desolate scenes because a lifeless environment draws us into its eery stillness. Life is cheerless without the touch of a loving hand, the assuring words of a friend, the comforting smile of an understanding colleague, or without the rustle of a child's play. We could own a whole country but be joyless because there is no one with whom to share it. We would love our wealth, yet languish from the lack of love. Personally and emotionally we need each other. Why, then, is it so difficult to form the kinds of interpersonal bonds that bind us in the types of relationship that meet these needs?

Most people believe there are many types of human relationships. But from my years of work as a clergyman, psychotherapist, and psychologist, I have learned that the types of relationships are neither as numerous nor as complex as we might think. When, for example, you entertain private thoughts, make a purchase at the market, help a stranger seeking directions, participate in an activity with a friend, and tenderly embrace a loved one, you share in the total range of relationships.

When we know what people want, we know their reason for relating. And we understand the relationship pattern that unfolds. People relate with one another to receive some benefit from their interaction. If a conflict occurs, their relationship can break down before they get the benefit. Because divergent views cause the conflict, they argue to change one another's perceptions, hoping to resolve their differences with clarifications and earnest persuasion. Typically, by making some concessions and acknowledging misunderstandings, they may reach an accord, but usually with misgivings and a confusing sense of loss. The relationship is restored, but its character seems flawed.

Entangled in our differences, we lose sight of the bond that brought us together. When we analyze conflicts we learn that they don't originate from differences but from our use of inappropriate relationship bonds. Or they are caused by appropriate bonds we use wrongly and, many times, deceptively. Conflicts develop when we conceal our motives, telling others what we want them to believe. Then we confuse them with behaviors that dispute what we have said. They reflect their confusion by attacking us. We, in turn, fight them off with denials and distracting arguments. Following lengthy and emotional exchanges, we reach an uneasy truce. But a completely satisfactory resolution of differences is seldom achieved. And we are left to continue the relationship with distrust and righteous indignation.

To understand why some relationships flourish while others are plagued by discord, we need to examine them in terms of their bondings. In any troubled relationship the involved parties have bound themselves together, each using a different bond.

INTRAPERSONAL RELATIONSHIPS

The Self-Bond

As you read this book, your immediate environment and your thoughts and feelings are your life space. If you move to another room and become engaged in another activity, you are in a different environment with different thoughts and feelings. In each situation you are in the center of your life space (Figure 1).

Figure 1 – The Intrapersonal Relationship

35

We are not always alone in our life space. We have many reasons for asking other people to come into it, or they invite themselves into it. At times we can control the privacy of our life space. Usually we cannot. The gregarious person leaves the door wide open to his life space. The reclusive individual guards it zealously.

At times we lock ourselves away from other people to reflect and think. Our reflections may lead us through the most recent events of the day, or carry us into the remote past to experience again a happy time or to feel once more an emotional pain. This is a journey into the "person" of the self, and along the way we discover more of who we are. At these times we relate *intrapersonally*. The mind conducts its own dialogue, commonly referred to as "talking to the self" - a relationship of self interacting with self. Generally, we enter into a self-relationship to struggle with a problem, or to gain some new understanding of our personal and emotional life.

We perceive "closed personalities" - people who are "wrapped up in themselves" most of the time - to be stable, in control of their lives, and free from stress and anxiety. On the other hand, we view excessively self-disclosing individuals, who openly share their troubling thoughts and feelings, to be unstable. Experience teaches us that these generalizations are erroneous. Both introverts and extroverts can have disabling personal or emotional problems. They differ only in how they manage them, intrapersonally or interpersonally.

The question isn't whether or not to relate intrapersonally. Rather, the question is, "How frequently do we want to become involved in this type of relating?" Periodically, everyone needs the respite of silence and solitude.

Those who have many associations with others don't have absorbing intrapersonal lives. They give their time, energy, and

36

attention to relationships with people who, like themselves, enjoy various forms of give-and-take. They are happiest when relating interpersonally, and least happy when not sharing their lives.

Individuals, on the other hand, who have few contacts with others are vigorously active intrapersonally. Their activity can be a lengthy monologue delivered to self or a series of fleeting thoughts that they briefly entertain and quickly dismiss. Many people choose to relate with themselves and make it an exclusive style of living. "Timid souls," for example, can have intense inner longings to associate with others but, for various reasons, fear interpersonal relationships. Their interpersonal relationships, therefore, take the form of fantasy in which personal threats have been removed. They are unhappy in the loneliness of their isolation. Still, they aren't willing to risk relating to others, even to test the reality of the fear that confines them.

If we take intrapersonal relating to an extreme, we remove ourselves almost entirely from the company of others. The cloistered monk or the reclusive hermit chooses the self as their living companion. For them, solitary living is satisfying because the ends it serves can be achieved in no other way.

Many do not have the option to relate or not to relate to self. They are forced to relate intrapersonally by circumstances which they can't control. Drug addicts who have surrendered to their dependency, and have abandoned duty or trust, become strangers to all except themselves. Because they are irresponsible and unreliable, they alienate everyone around them. Avoidance and censure from others drives them even further into their seclusion.

The seriously mentally ill have even fewer choices in their relationship patterns. Unable to grasp reality outside of themselves, they are compelled to connect with the only realities they can know - those created within. Try as we might, we can't draw them into meaningful relationships in the world from which they are detached.

Relating intrapersonally can be invigorating. Alone, reflecting on life, we restore a sense of self through introspective contemplations. We recharge our depleted emotional energy. We become spiritually renewed and thereby more comfortable in stressful interactions with other people.

Self-with-self relationship building is a useful daily energizing activity.

EGOCENTRIC RELATIONSHIPS

The Desire/Need Bond

At the first level of relating beyond self, we approach others to secure something from them. Self-seeking brings us together for a mutually agreeable transaction. We would not engage in the relationship except for the urging of a personal need or a desire that we expect to be fulfilled.

The word that best describes an egocentric relationship is "functional." It functions to enable me to get something that I would otherwise not have. In egocentric relationships I satisfy my desires/needs by *using* other people. In the quest to fulfill a desire/need the "I" obscures the other person who simply becomes a "you." Using people as objects to get something we want is a form of abasement. Their value to us is determined by what they can do for us. The primitive character in this type of relationship is apparent.

Two individuals create an egocentric relationship by meeting to form a life space common to them (Figure 2). They

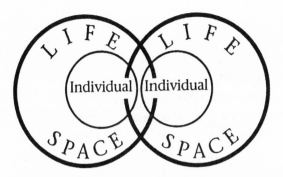

Figure 2. The Egocentric Relationship

maintain it long enough to make their exchange, and in many instances never come together again. They do not bring their whole selves to the interaction. And both come from a larger and more permanent life space to meet together and complete their "business" with each other.

Our society recognizes and accepts egocentric relationships as an acceptable way of fulfilling desires and needs. It is, for example, the bond between the producer and the consumer. Workers with specific skills make products which we, the consumers, desire. We also buy services from providers such as physicians, lawyers, funeral directors, hairdressers, automotive mechanics, and clergymen. They receive money, and we receive service. Beyond this, we don't need each other.

The desire/need-bond is used almost exclusively within our political and economic system. Stockholders own large industries and invest their money to earn a profit. Management, representing the owners, hires laborers to manufacture the product. The agreement is straight forward. Workers state, "We will work for you if you will pay us a wage equal to the value of our services." They form labor unions to guarantee that the compensation is equitable for the work performed. Management and labor "use" each other for the benefits each receives

- products for the managers, and wages for the workers. It is an honorable alliance in which two groups openly and deliberately treat one another as objects for the fulfillment of their desires and needs.

In every election year most of us use the desire/need-bond to unite with political candidates. Individuals seeking public office promise to work to achieve the goals which they believe their constituents desire. People respond by voting for these office seekers. Their expectation: *votes have purchase value.* Cynics scoff at the candidate's deceit and the electorate's gullibility. But the relationship thrives because of the selfishness of each.

Individual contacts are usually absent from egocentric relationships between large groups. In labor and management negotiations, a few trusted persons represent each group at the bargaining table. Or, on the campaign circuit, the candidate presents himself and his platform on television, in newspapers, and to gatherings at political rallies and banquets. The two parties, candidate and elector, have no need to relate because the goals they seek can be attained without personally interacting.

Relationships founded upon desire/need are easy to manage because they are simple and direct. Each person looks for a good deal. Personal familiarity and friendship play no role in the exchange. The shopper who purchases a dress does not wish to know the clerk behind the counter who receives and places her money in the cash register. The exchange is not one of personal intimacy. It is one of money for clothing. Although pleasant greetings may be exchanged, the entire transaction can be carried out without a smile or a word passing between them.

Relating egocentrically is an outgrowth of the profit motive and consumer orientation to which the majority of people have

40

adapted, particularly over the last half century. Treating ourselves to whatever we desire/need by using another person is widely practiced, particularly in materialistic societies such as The United States. Because it is not possible to invest personally and emotionally in the life of every person with whom we have a business transaction, most of our relationships are like this.

Using people as objects has prompted government agencies to pass legislation requiring honesty in merchandising products and services. "Warnings" are printed on cigarette packages. All commercially produced foods contain a listing of ingredients. Over the counter drugs carry labels describing use, cautions, and side effects. Automobile mechanics, hairdressers, physicians, and lawyers must be licensed. The license warrants that they are trained and professionally qualified to deliver the services they offer. These measures protect consumers from fraud. They are needed because consumers lack knowledge about most products and services. Although protective regulations control some egocentric relationships, in most encounters we are wise to stand by the adage, "Let the buyer beware."

In egocentric relationships we are responsible for protecting our own interest. We give only in order to get. Fairness is not a guiding principle in determining either the quantity or quality of the products or services that we exchange.

ALTRUISTIC RELATIONSHIPS

The Charity Bond

Altruism is an unselfish concern for others expressed either as a gift or a service. In the altruistic relationship, one person recognizes another's need, and, having the desire and ability to satisfy the need, responds appropriately. Whether solicited or not, the altruistic individual moves toward the person needing help with the question, "How can I help you?" It is a relationship of giver and receiver. The giver shares the gift and does not ask, "What will I get in return?"

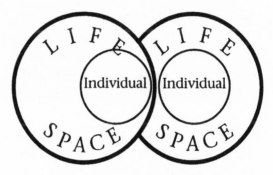

Figure 3. The Altruistic Relationship

The helping person enters the life space of the "needy" person (Figure 3) but shares none of her personal life. The receiving person, on the other hand, opens her personal life, detailing the nature of her needs or problems. The person with the need is central in the lives of both persons in the relationship.

When distress in the life of one person arouses compassion in another, the setting is created for an altruistic relationship. The creed that directs the work of charity states, "I will be for you what you need me to be. I ask only that you allow me to give to you."

Charitable people give to those in need but don't share emotionally with them. Although benefactors are sensitive to the emotional needs of people whose lives they try to uplift, they do not become entangled in their despair and cheerless spirit. They know how to be genuinely sensitive and warm-hearted, how to be caring without becoming engulfed in the emotional trappings of those they serve.

Because there has never been enough public money to fund services for all indigent persons in our society, we rely heavily upon people to come to one another's aid. Civilized societies understand that the prosperity of all is endangered by the misery of the downtrodden. Oppressed people rise up and demand a fair share of the bounty.

From its founding, America has been lauded for its benevolence to people and nations in need. But strangely, when the need of a person at our elbow requires us to commit our "selves," not merely contribute our money or material goods, our altruism is not always strong enough to arouse us to action.

However, we are seeing some signs of change. There is evidence that the adult generation, particularly people from their mid-thirties to late forties, are beginning to voluntarily reach out to the less fortunate. Nearly 50 percent of the respondents in a recently published Gallup Poll said they do charity or volunteer work. This is an increase of 19 percent over an earlier Gallup survey on the same question. An estimated 90 million American volunteers give an average of three and one-half hours each week in service to others. And the value of these services could total $110 billion annually.

While it is encouraging that people in their early middle-age are becoming more charitable with their money and time, it is disheartening to learn that the generation following has little concern for the helpless. The National Task Force on Higher Education in its 1988 "Report to the Campus" states that students see social problems simply as abstractions in the larger society beyond the campus.

Dr. Gary H. Quehl, president of the Council for the Advancement and Support of Education, writes, "On the one hand, we see students who are eager and energetic, possessing enormous potential. But they are so self-centered that they are immune to the world around them. They have yet to be asked to extend themselves to anyone or anything beyond themselves. They are inward looking and lack a public service mentality. Indeed, they possess almost no understanding of the essential truth about America discovered long ago by Alexis de Tocqueville - that we prosper individually only as we put something back into society for the common good."[1]

Without altruism, the moral quality of our communities would be characterized by heartless neglect of helpless people. Volunteer firemen, ambulance and emergency medical services would be gone. Children deprived of a relationship with a loving father or mother would not have "Big Brothers" and "Big Sisters" to care for them. There would be no men and women to coach youth athletic teams. Community food banks, meals on wheels, religious charities, and aid to disaster victims could not be provided without the individuals who compassionately give to human need. Gone, too, would be fairs, carnivals, and parades which offer festive respites from life's stresses, and service activities of the Lions, Rotary and Kiwanis Clubs which reach out to give assistance to the infirm and disabled. Society would find it financially prohibitive to purchase the services that are given by its charitable citizens. Our greatest gift is the love to give.

PERSONAL RELATIONSHIPS

The Similarity Bond

At still another level of relating, we share part of ourselves with others in a common life space. We open our personal lives for them to see and know (Figure 4).

Figure 4 – The Personal Relationship

Personality traits, value systems, and interest patterns are important considerations in personal relationships, since they involve people who tend to be like each other. Their similarities are the bond that ties them together in a personal union.

In personal relationships individuals relate as equals, giving and taking. Each is free to differ and confront, but not with malice or intimidation. And the relationship is mutual. We cannot harmoniously sustain personal relationships if the responsibility for maintaining them is shifted to one person. A personal relationship is mutually rewarding only when we invest mutually in its nurture.

45

As good friends, we share in each other's joys and misfortunes. We value each other as persons and do not use our relationship for selfish ends. We respond cheerfully to requests for help, giving time, energy, and skills as a privilege, not as a burdensome chore. Two individuals in a personal relationship understand that they are special to each other. Their lives are enriched in their personal associations, because they know they have a preferred place in each other's life.

Personal relationships are formed on three different levels of familiarity. At the most common level is the casual meeting in which two individuals speak to each other using first names. They are likely to greet one another with, "How are you?" or, "What's new with you?" The conversation may then expand into common areas of interest. Although they do not reveal their inner lives to each other, they do share personal opinions and views.

Casual friends relate when paths cross. Coming upon one another on the street, in a grocery market, or at a social event they pause long enough to chat about some light-hearted topic. The mood is buoyant and free from emotional and personal tension.

We feel personally uplifted when we share a kindred spirit with many different people. Our casual friendships help us avoid the aloneness and estrangement of those who are friendless and trapped within the emptiness of their intrapersonal isolation. Casual friendships provide that little touch of spice that sees us through the vexations of each day and keeps us from falling into the permanent clutches of the "blues."

When friends become our companions, we move to the second level of personal relating. At this level we are personal associates, openly disclosing ourselves and sharing life experiences. Our personalities mesh, creating a smooth flow of harmonious interactions.

Associate friends share in golf outings, shopping sprees, vacations, social events, and informal gatherings. The pleasures of their activities are enhanced by their affectionate, mutual personal regard. Activities draw them into their relationship, and help them enjoy each other's personality.

Associate friendships are fewer because they require a larger investment of time and energy than casual relationships. Because time and energy are limited, we carefully select those few people most similar to ourselves. All others in whom we may take some pleasure remain casual friends.

If the similarities that draw us into an associate friendship change, our relationship either becomes casual or is severed completely. As friends, we no longer feel comfortable with each other. Nor do we find our experiences together personally satisfying. When the bond is altered, the relationship is correspondingly changed.

A Changed Relationship: Kathy

Kathy and her husband of 20 years were friends of a married couple in another state. Several times yearly they visited each other to share in weekend parties and social activities. Over the years Kathy became addicted to alcohol. Because I had provided marital therapy for her and her husband some years earlier, she came to me for treatment of her addiction. When her attempt to control the use of alcohol with moderate drinking failed, she decided to abstain entirely from its use.

Following several months of sobriety, Kathy found it increasingly easy to be content with non-alcoholic beverages. Her husband and friends continued their drinking patterns. Surprisingly, she discovered that her friends were becoming less interesting and less fun to be with. She wished for weekends with these friends to pass quickly so she could be alone and involved in activities which she felt were more pleasant and satisfying. In the same way, although confusing to her, Kathy felt somewhat estranged from her husband whose drinking and lifestyle had not changed.

She took up her college studies with more enthusiasm. And she found the simple pleasures of church work and family gatherings, previously peripheral attractions, to be personally enriching. As Kathy underwent change in her life, she searched for new friends whose values and interest patterns were closer to those she was developing.

From Kathy's experience we learn that the bond which unites people in associate friendships is only as strong as the similarities that attract them. When likenesses erode, the friendship languishes and is replaced with a memory.

At the highest level of personal relating, we share problems, secrets and intimate thoughts. We become close hand-and-glove friends, trusted confidants. We use confidant relationships to share our emotional distress when, alone, we do not feel strong enough to bear its pain. We choose our confidants from among those friends whom we have concluded to be the most caring and most understanding.

When one friend feels low, the other becomes the "counselor" who listens patiently and offers understanding with reassuring words and gestures. The friend in distress talks openly about her thoughts or feelings. She knows her confidante will use these personal disclosures only to assist in easing her emotional discomfort. Although the conditions that created the *low feelings* do not change, the burden is lighter because it is shared by two people.

When distress is greater than our capacity to endure, and we have no confidant with whom to share, we turn to non-productive methods to cope with our anguish. Giving in to feelings of helplessness, we may isolate ourselves and suffer passively. Or we may anesthetize ourselves with drugs or alcohol. And, if desperate with no sense of hope, we may decide that suicide is the only way to end our hurt. A confidant at these times is the light at the end of the tunnel. He guides us through the darkness of our despair and into the brightness of optimism and joy. The message we hear from our confidant is simple: "Be still, I am with you."

Also, we call upon confidants to assist us when we try to sort out the pieces of a complex situation. Confidants help us to clarify the issues and give us insightful suggestions. They enable us to complete the decision-making process with a higher level of certainty.

Confidants not only share common personal traits, values, and interests, they also act similarly to handle situations and problems. Males are likely to deal with them cognitively with emotional detachment while females tend to internalize them and relate to them emotionally and cognitively detached. Consequently, individuals most often create confidant relationships with someone of the same sex.

LOVE RELATIONSHIPS

The Love Bond

The most intimate and emotionally enriching level of relating is when two people occupy the focal position in the life of the other. Their love for each other is greater than the love each has for the self. The overlap of their selves, as well as the overlap of their life spaces, is more extensive than in any other relationship. It becomes even further extended as love deepens. (Figure 5).

Figure 5 – Love Relationships

Two people in a love relationship devote themselves to each other's well-being. Time assigned to self, when needed or requested, is given readily to the beloved. The good fortunes of each are mutually shared. The sufferings of one become the sufferings of both. Together they feel joy, sadness, elation, anger, and frustration even though the experiences that create these emotions happen to only one of them. Their devotion is a living pledge and if written would say, "As you have placed me in the center of your life, so have I given you the central position in my life."

Come Into My Life

The cost of loving is not calculated before it is put to work for the loved one. Loving isn't restrained. It always responds to the internal coercion created by the loveliness of the one who is to receive it. Although a lover receives the same quantity and quality of love that is given, his loving is not conditioned by reciprocity. Each is secure in knowing that the love which flows between them will not stop. And while the delight is in being loved, the honor is in loving.

In addition to the strong heartfelt emotion in love-bonded relationships, love is equally present in the *minds* of lovers. Each has clearly identified the beautiful traits that makes the other so lovely. Their love is more than blind infatuation or romantic fantasy. It is passionate and affectionate because of those personal, physical and emotional attributes that have taken command of their love.Here are three examples of love-bonded relationships: We have read historical accounts of the slave who, when freed, chose to remain with his master. They were bonded in a love stronger than the decree abolishing slavery. The love of Jonathan for David was stronger than the bond of blood which he severed to protect the life of his beloved friend from the wrath of his father, King Saul.[2] Gayle Sayers, the outstanding former running back of the Chicago Bears loved Brian Piccolo, his fellow team member who died from cancer. His love was stronger than the difference of their skin color. These relationships, and others like them, grow from a seed of love nurtured by the ardor of personal devotion two people share.

Of all love relationships, none so totally appeals to our imagination as the deep and sincere devotion of a man and a woman in love in marriage. Marriage ties them together after they have united with a bond of love sealed with selfless

51

devotion. The most esteemed gift and the highest honor that a human being can receive is to be invited to live in the center of another person's life. In their alliance of love, husband and wife offer this gift and honor to each other.

In a relationship of married lovers there is room only for each other within their undivided affection. This is the solemn pledge that a bride and groom make with the poetic beauty of their marriage vows, in the presence of God, family, and friends. In the marriage ceremony they declare that no other person will sit on the lofty throne of love which they have reserved for one another.

In their love relationship, a married couple holds no love in reserve. Commitment is complete. They give all their love. And they experience giving love as pleasure equal to receiving it. Because love is all-consuming, laying claim to the mind's reverie and the heart's beat, no one is capable of having more than one such relationship.

Love has always been a popular theme for writers and poets. Theatre owes its appeal in large part to its treatment of love - love betrayed and dishonored, love cheapened and made vulgar, love possessed and allowed to slip away, love proposed and rejected, and love lost but recovered. Love is depicted as sweet words, unbridled passion, a bearer of gifts, and acts of mercy. Although love is each of these, it is more than all of these. Love is the devotion of myself to another whom I have chosen to cherish more than self.

Regretfully, love is easily idealized and so very difficult to practice. At the moment of marriage a bride and groom declare that their love will prevail against all the forces that lay in wait to destroy it. Yet, how quickly the rapture of that moment can fade and be replaced with a spiritless routine of emotional strangers living together. Disillusioned with the crumbling of the "dream marriage," they mourn love's passing from their relationship.

I have learned from years of therapy with married couples that their love is usually still intact, even when loving behaviors and words have diminished. When I question them, as I always do, about their love, both spouses say, perhaps with hesitation, "Oh yes, I still love him/her." Yet, their angry conflicts contradict these affirmations.

I find that husbands and wives who come to me for help usually have appraised their feelings accurately. They have love for each other, but they can't use it because it is lost among the brambles of their interpersonal clashes. It cannot find an outlet through which to perform its work. That outlet is the bond of devotion to one another's loveliness, through which love always flows.

Healing the love-bond is the key to renewing a broken relationship, not just solving problems and resolving conflicts. When the bond of devotion to loveliness is replaced with one of the other bonds I have discussed, deliberately or not, the love relationship cannot survive. Egocentricity is nearly always the bond that is substituted for the bond of loving devotion. Through small degrees of behavioral change, slowly but surely, individuals reinsert themselves in the center of their own lives. The role of the love relationship therapist, then, is to help them rediscover the loveliness of one another and rebuild their bond of devoted loving.

If individuals in each type of relationship I have described always used the appropriate bond, they would have few interpersonal conflicts. Disagreements that do occur certainly wouldn't cause a major rupture in their relationships. Most people, however, have relationship breakdowns because they blend different bonds or use a bond unsuitable for their goals.

Now we'll discuss the many ways in which we use "crossed-bondings" and the confusion and disharmony they produce.

CHAPTER FOUR

Relationships With Crossed-Bondings

when we build different bridges, we can't meet to make satisfying exchanges in our relationship

Sometime ago a colleague shared with me an ethical dilemma which she confronted for the first time as a counselor. She spoke slowly, censuring herself for what she considered a personal weakness - falling in love with a male patient. She had always practiced ethically and with sound professional judgement. Now she was upset by her failure to control the strong feelings of attraction for the twenty-five-year-old man she saw weekly for therapy. The question she asked reflected her disappointment, "How could this happen to me?"

Although contrary to the popular stereotype, psychotherapists are human; they have values, biases, personal, and emotional needs. In addition to the knowledge and skills they bring to their professional practice, they also bring the whole of their humanness. Yet, therapists are expected to control their needs and drives. They cannot permit them to interfere with the psychotherapeutic process.

Fortunately, my colleague did not transgress ethical boundaries or compromise her professional integrity. Aware of the need awakened in her, she understood that ethically she could not use a patient to gratify her desires. She candidly discussed her feelings with the patient and arranged for him to be referred to my care. In this case the patient was not personally harmed and the therapist preserved both her professional reputation and her self-respect.

Some therapists will argue that her counter-transference feelings should have been analyzed as an integral part of their therapeutic relationship. I don't want to discuss here the merits of any particular technique which therapists use to resolve professional relationships issues. Rather, I have cited this situation to illustrate how the character of a relationship is notably altered when one bond is replaced with another.

When this man came to her, she understood clearly that she was the "helping person" and he was the emotionally-troubled patient seeking help. In the early stages, she and the patient were bound together in an altruistic relationship. She put aside her personal and emotional needs to attend to his needs only.

With the emergence of counter-transference feelings, the therapeutic focus moved from the patient to the therapist. The relationship was no longer altruistic. The needs of one individual, the patient, were no longer the only concern in the relationship. With her own need pushed to the forefront, the therapist ceased to be the selfless altruist and provided only an awkward simulation of true therapy.

If she had continued to provide treatment using her bond of need, which had replaced the giving of herself, the patient would have been removed from the center of her attention. He would have soon noticed the shift from their concerted effort to resolve his issues to the therapist's subtle insinuation of herself into his psychological space. Forced to share the therapeutic focus, his sense of self would be threatened, giving rise to anger and frustration. Movement in therapy would be interrupted as treatment is directed from the patient's needs to the conflict created by his estranged relationship with the therapist.

Most people relate to others with little understanding of the type of bond that brings them together. Consequently, conflicts develop when the contending parties don't receive the gratifications they expect. They argue about what is right or just, failing to recognize the root of their discord - the bond through which they are relating.

When my colleague injected her personal need into the treatment process, the relationship became impure. She, now related egocentrically, and without her patient's awareness and sanction. He fully believed that they were meeting to discuss only his needs and problems. She changed the relationship by allowing her bond of personal need, under the guise of charity, to direct the flow of therapy. With the development of a *crossed-bonding* there was no longer a singleness of purpose.

Crossed-bondings always result in crossed-purposes. They occur when one person in a relationship introduces another bond without the other's knowledge and consent. Conflict arises and, if not resolved, the party that feels betrayed dissolves the relationship. A relationship that doesn't serve the purposes of the participants cannot be sustained.

Often individuals deliberately create crossed-bonded relationships to achieve selfish ends. They deceive the unsuspecting persons, concealing from them the real purpose of the relationship. Examples of this concept follow later in this chapter.

Crossed-bondings also develop within relationships that were established first with a single bond known and accepted by both parties. I have described in the therapeutic relationship at the beginning of this chapter the process by which this change can occur. The therapist, in this instance, entered the relationship with her male patient to help him understand and gain control of his life. When her personal need surfaced, undivided attention could not be maintained and her original mission yielded to self-preoccupation. Her bond of personal need replaced the original bond of charitable concern. The relationship for her switched from altruism to egocentricity.

There are many combinations of relationships created by crossed-bondings (Figure 6). On the following pages I describe several examples for each combination. Reflecting on these relationships, readers will recognize many similar ones in which they have shared, or with which they are familiar.

EGOCENTRIC - ALTRUISTIC RELATIONSHIPS (EA)

Someone who receives compassionate help from another person does not always know if the charity is an honest expression of caring. It may be prompted by the other person's selfishness.

Troubled people, because they are usually helpless and have few resources, are vulnerable to manipulation by self-serving people. Unprincipled individuals look for such people and reach out, in the guise of charity, to relieve them from their trouble. In these instances they use "charity" to serve themselves.

Come Into My Life

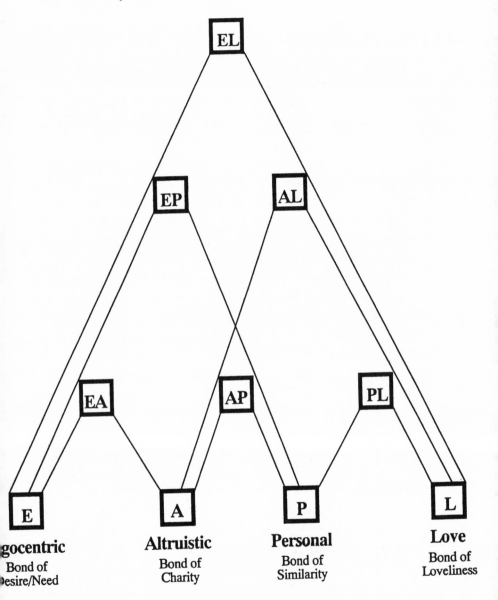

Figure 6 – Crossed-Bondings

59

Desperate for deliverance from their personal, emotional, spiritual, or physical discomfort, needy people generally do not question the motivation of "healers" who offer help. The media constantly report stories about helpless people who fall prey to predatory solicitations of the proverbial "wolves in sheeps' clothing."

The PTL religious empire collapsed when the multi-million dollar life style of its founder, Jimmy Bakker, was exposed. Tens of thousands of men and women who trusted him to minister to their spiritual needs had financed his "charitable" organization. They learned, only after his duplicity was unveiled, that the altruism of his spiritual offerings was a facade behind which he concealed greed.

Television "crusaders for Christ" make wide appeals to their disciples for money. They do so, insisting that their ministries relieve spiritually afflicted people from their burdens of guilt and despair. They tell their trusting followers that money is needed to spread the message of life and salvation to those hungering after righteousness. People dead in sin are most vulnerable to the deception of the religious altruist who offers to save them.

Powerful nations routinely use the gift of charity to exploit weaker nations. The United States and the former Soviet Union built their friendships with the world's poorer nations by giving them industrial, medical, military, and food supplies. They gave the aid in exchange for a commitment to their own political ideology. If these dependent nations changed their political ideologies, the aid was withdrawn.

Closer to home, people engage in egocentric-altruistic relationships for a variety of reasons. We respect the father who contributes his time to manage a little league baseball team, and applaud him for his generosity. Then we learn that he does so because he can use his position as manager to assure that his son, with limited athletic ability, will be in the starting lineup.

How often have we read about or known people who tend to the needs of an elderly widow living nearby. They are solicitous about her health and general welfare, provide transportation, run errands, cook meals, and make minor repairs on her house. Not so apparent to those who laud their altruism is the egocentric nature of the relationship. They use charity to induce the widow, who has no relatives, to leave her wealth to them.

An example of an egocentric altruistic relationship I recall from my work as a high school guidance counselor involved three teenagers who befriended a socially isolated student. Several of the teachers in the school commended the boys for opening their circle to a forlorn peer. What the teachers didn't know was that the boys extended their kindly invitation because their new friend had an automobile and willingly chauffeured them around town. Had they known, their commendation would have turned to censure.

Because the needy person is vulnerable and the egocentric person is greedy, the relationship leads to exploitation. Unless the greed is exposed, the relationship continues with all of its deceptive trappings. When it is unmasked, the exploited individual feels cheapened. The self-serving person, on the other hand, insists that the charitable actions were sincere and honorable.

EGOCENTRIC-PERSONAL RELATIONSHIPS (EP)

Many people have a free and relaxing manner of relating to others. They like people and enjoy being with them in activities

in which they share their personalities naturally and spontaneously. They tend to be trusting, making it tempting for others
to draw them into relationships and use them to fulfill their
selfish needs or desires.

These people are easy victims for anyone who uses the bond
of similarity fraudulently. By demonstrating similar interests,
values and beliefs, a selfish person lures the trusting individual
into his self-serving trap. He does and says the things which
make him appear to be "cut from the same mold." His message
is, "See, I am like you. You can trust me."

Egocentric-personal relationships are so common that we
don't consider them malicious or even dishonest. They are used
skillfully by those who deliberately deceive, and intuitively by
others for whom it makes sense to identify with the person who
can give them something they want. For example, the high
school teacher, who is the chairperson of the student scholarship committee suddenly finds himself in a friendship with a
prominent community businessman. Knowing the teacher is a
fan of the local professional football team, the businessman
invites him to the next Sunday's game. Their personal relationship continues for several months before the teacher realizes
that the businessman is using him to lobby for his daughter to
receive a scholarship.

We're familiar with the tactics of a university athletic
recruiter. Pursuing an unusually talented athlete, the recruiter
is careful not to offend either the athlete or his parents. Antici-
pating their concerns, he gives the answers before their questions are asked. He speaks persuasively about his concern for
their son's education: "We monitor the academic performance
of all players throughout the season; tutors are always available
at no cost; if necessary, your son can be excused from practice

to study with a tutor for major exams; he will have special housing with quiet study facilities; we'll be here to help your son work through any problems" - and more.

The recruiter's manner is affable, relaxed and warm. He is personable, and his message is clear, "I am more than just your coach, I am your friend." He depends as much upon his friendship to get the athlete to sign on the dotted line as he does on the quality of the athletic organization or the excellence of the academic offerings. The young athlete and his parents ask, "How can we turn down such a nice man?"

"Would you buy a used car from this guy?" is both a humorous question and a serious statement about the integrity of people who sell cars. Car salesmen are adept at developing egocentric-personal relationships. They use these relationships as privileged trusts to talk customers into buying automobiles. They draw customers into their confidence with handshakes, smiles and first name familiarity. They express interest in the customer's family, neighborhood, and hobbies. Often, customers buy the automobile as much in response to the salesman's personality as to their belief in the excellence of the car.

When the daughter doesn't receive the scholarship, the business friend greets the teacher coldly. The athlete who doesn't fulfill the coach's expectations is dismissed from the team and is hardly acknowledged when he and the coach run into each other on campus. And at the local automobile show, the car salesman gives only a weak nod of the head as he walks by the customer who didn't buy his sales pitch. When their expectations were not fulfilled these individuals withdrew their friendships.

Because we respond positively to warmth and friendliness, personal charm is more forceful than reason. A poignant commentary on the power of charisma is the phrase, "He could sell a refrigerator to an Eskimo."

Slippery-tongued politicians, flamboyant television evangelists, con artists, and occult gurus attract followers because their winsome personalities make them believable when their messages are bogus. When we identify personally with the character of others, we are vulnerable to their deceit. And we learn too late that personal relationships we make in haste often turn out to be egocentrically motivated by those who use us and then drop us by the wayside.

ALTRUISTIC-PERSONAL RELATIONSHIPS (AP)

People with kind hearts often discover that others misinterpret their expressions of kindness. Needy persons, and also friendless, are most likely to make such poor judgements. They become personally attracted to the altruistic givers and seize the opportunity to use the "personal relationship" to lift them from loneliness.

Altruistic individuals offer kindness, not the gift of self. They expect their generous assistance to be received as a *gift from me*, not a *gift of me*. But friendless people often want friendship even more than relief from their distress. Given the depth of that personal need, they reasonably infer that kindness from another is also friendship.

Scripts for war dramas frequently include a sub-plot about a soldier and a native boy who become involved in an unexpected relationship. Usually the soldier and the boy come together in a hazardous situation. With affectionate regard, he befriends his young associate with candy. At this point, the soldier expects the relationship to end. Although he urges the boy to go away, he simply disappears for a little while, only to reappear later. He wants to stay with *his new friend.*

An altruistic-personal relationship is created when a businessman hires the father of a destitute family, and the father interprets employment as an invitation to friendship. And so he not only tells his new employer all about himself, he also questions him about his personal and family life. Pressed by his need for friendship, the father is not aware that the businessman considers his inquiries an intrusion into his private life.

The volunteer for meals on wheels is an easy target for an altruistic-personal relationship. Several times daily she is interrupted by phone calls from the elderly widow to whom she delivers a noon meal. The lonely widow has interpreted the volunteer's kind interest as an invitation for friendship. Her phone calls are a veiled request to the volunteer to "please be my friend."

For all of these needy individuals the desire to relate personally with their benefactors is as compelling as the need for the relief that comes with their charity. The young waif, the unemployed father, and the lonely widow may be able to find other ways to have their immediate needs met. But finding someone who wants to give friendship is much more difficult.

When I give altruistically, I have fulfilled my obligation. Having delivered the gift or service, the moral injunction within me to share my good fortune is assuaged.

When I give myself in a personal relationship, I am bound to a continuing commitment. This is the mark of friendship: two people readily and cheerfully available to each other because they are personally similar.

There is no bond of similarity, however, to hold two people together in an altruistic-personal relationship. The altruist in this relationship is, therefore, in the uncomfortable position of resisting the unwelcomed personal advances of the needy and friendless person.

To avoid this personal conflict, benefactors frequently choose to give anonymously or hire someone to provide the needed service. Desiring only to meet human need, they want no public acknowledgment of their generosity, and they expect no gratitude.

Neither person in an altruistic-personal relationship intends to deceive the other. One wants to relieve an affliction; the other wants a friendship. Conflict arises when the giver considers the relationship terminated, and the receiver pushes for its continuation. The altruistic person tries to resolve the conflict by retreating from the relationship, but is pursued by the beneficiary.

Although altruistic-personal relationships are not formally dissolved, over time they wither because they are nurtured only by one of two persons. Needy people, in time, drop their entreaties if repeatedly turned away.

ALTRUISTIC-LOVE RELATIONSHIPS (AL)

Altruistic-love relationships are similar to altruistic-personal relationships. They differ only in the depth of intimacy which needy people attempt to develop with those who assist them. More than personal friendship, they want and seek love. The message to their benefactor is, "Let me become a special person in your life. Center your thoughts, activities, and attention in me."

Clergymen frequently are involved in altruistic-love relationships, for example, when ministering to individuals grieving the death of a family member. Their compassion leaves them vulnerable to emotional seduction by the bereaved. Repeated visits by a clergyman with a recent widow provides consolation and fills a personal and emotional void. While the loss of love and intimacy can't be replaced with comforting words and scripture, a grieving widow finds in her clergyman the love that was abruptly taken from her. At this time in her life, she construes his attention as personal affection and emotional attachment. It is no small task for him, then, to tactfully refuse her amorous advances without adding to her despair. For she will perceive his rejection as yet another loss to be grieved.

When it is time for children, temporarily placed in foster homes, to be moved to a permanent residence, they often resist leaving their foster parents. Although these substitute parents may feel deeply affectionate toward their foster children, they do not, in most instances, feel binding love. Still, because they need love, these children perceive custodial guardianship as loving attention. When separation occurs, therefore, foster parents feel sadness, but these children grieve the loss of love.

It is difficult to convince beneficiaries in altruistic-love relationships that their kind helpers do not love them in the way that they want to be loved. Because their longing for love is so pressing, they don't understand that a love relationship is not practical. They meet every reason with a counter argument, and when these relationships end, needy persons feel forsaken and again cheated by life. Trust levels go down, and they retreat a little further into the safety of intrapersonal isolation.

Millions of people in our society have concern and compassion for the physically and emotionally destitute. Moved by sympathy, they offer to help them. Although they mean well, these kindly helpers generally are not prepared to deal with the intensity of the affection that their benevolence can evoke. They learn that by responding to a painfully human condition they may also awaken a gripping need for love which they cannot fulfill.

If altruists carefully define their role when aiding needy people, much of the misunderstanding that occurs is avoided. "Helping persons" are responsible for structuring the "helping relationship." They should explain clearly why they are helping, what help they can give, and how they plan to provide that help. Their charity does not include the gift of self. But they can listen lovingly to understand the loneliness and emotional seclusion of the lives that are opened to them. We all find comfort in being understood, even if the compassionate understanding doesn't lessen our suffering.

PERSONAL-LOVE RELATIONSHIP (PL)

A relationship that begins as friendship becomes crossed-bonded when one individual develops a love attachment for the other. That person then wants to share more than interests and activities. He or she gives intimate devotion and expects to receive the same. In this relationship one is saying, "I am your friend," while the other asks, "Will you love me?"

Many people who relate as associate friends find their friendships imperceptibly changed when one becomes romantically attracted to the other. Personal-love relationships develop with disturbing regularity at every level of social interaction: secretary and boss, physician and nurse, male patron and female hairdresser, or two friends in any walk of life. With continuous contacts, they have many opportunities to seduce one another.

Working for years as the chairperson of a university's psychological services department, I have counseled female students who become romantically involved with male professors. Often, when this happens, the professors want only the friendships which evolve from friendly associations. The young women desire close and even intimate relationships.

Male college professors are cautioned about developing close personal friendships with their female students. But many feel they can do so without creating embarrassing conflicts for themselves or emotional confusion for their female friends. Their indiscretion generally results in charges of sexual harassment by their rejected youthful lovers. These professors are then left to defend their innocence and reputations.

It is common for married couples to share in mutually enjoyable activities with other couples. And, given the closeness of their relationships, one spouse may become physically and emotionally attracted to one of the other spouses. If a wife is unhappy with the emotional distance between herself and her husband, she may use these times of togetherness to lure another woman's husband into an intimate relationship. If happily married, he rejects her amorous advances. And, if her pursuit continues, she is inviting the break up of their personal relationship. If, on the other hand, he succumbs to her seduction, all friendships, as well as two marriages, are shattered.

Even a couple married for many years can find itself in a personal-love relationship. From my work with Randy and Gayle, I discovered how easily this can happen. She continued to love, but he allowed his relationship with her to drift into a confidential friendship.

Randy and Gayle

Randy and Gayle were married for 28 years and had two grown sons. By Gayle's account, the relationship with her husband was emotionally close for the first few years of their marriage. But as she became increasingly involved in her roles as a mother and homemaker, Randy invested more of his time in his career. In his leisure hours he played baseball in the local community league. As he grew older he chose to use his time to promote the athletic development of their youngest son. A fan of the local professional teams - baseball, football, basketball, and hockey - Randy either attended the games or watched them on television. If he was not absorbed in sports, he was busy puttering around the house or caring for the lawn. Randy and Gayle vacationed together, dined out alone or with other couples, attended social outings, and visited their families. But without loving nurture, their emotional and sexual relationship was neglected and lost its passion.

At age 47, with both sons gone from the home, Gayle sought to revive their love. She said they had no sex during the two years before her call for therapy. Randy, gently but forthrightly, rejected her love.

Gayle described Randy as a good husband, a loving father, a dutiful provider, never abusive, easy to please, and dedicated to the home and family. But he wasn't warm and affectionate. Randy openly acknowledged his reluctance to show feelings. Their active but separate lives had allowed him to emotionally distance himself from his wife.

At Gayle's insistence, Randy consented to therapy. Feeling comfortable with our relationship, Randy confided that he had always been sexually reticent with females. Now fifty years old, he confessed that his sex drive was nearly nonexistent. His wife's persistent appeals for sex only added to his anxieties and pushed him further into himself. He adamantly refused treatment for his sexual dysfunction. Yet, he didn't want to break up the marriage. He was content to share with his wife in the full range of activities that had always characterized their relationship. But he would not be the lover she wanted. Gayle asked him, "What will you do if I have an affair?" His reply was simple and direct, "What I don't know won't hurt me."

Randy terminated therapy and resumed his role as a committed friend in a personal relationship with his wife. Gayle remains in the home and occasionally comes to see me to explore options available to her. She can stay in the marriage and continue in a close friendship with her husband. As a cohabiting friend she may choose marital fidelity, or exercise the freedom to date other men. Or she can file for divorce and pursue a relationship with another man to find the mutual love she has been denied. The only viable option is the first one, since she would have to transgress her Christian values to exercise either of the latter two choices.

In personal-love relationships one individual gives friendship while the other gives love, and both are disappointed. The one who receives love wants only the commitment of friendship, and the one who is given friendship desires love.

EGOCENTRIC-LOVE RELATIONSHIPS (EL)

Egocentric-love relationships develop when a person uses love to secure a commitment, but doesn't want the love itself. A man, for example, uses love-like behaviors to evoke a truly loving response from a woman. But he doesn't want to win the woman's love. He wants only to secure something from her by using love as the lure to get it. With so many people hungering for warmth and affection, love is a powerful tool in the hands of unscrupulous people in their self-serving quests. It is effective because selfishness clothed with love is not easily detected.

Many bitter young women have come to me in my university setting, feeling emotionally torn by their egocentric-love relationships. The stories they relate are always the same. They began their relationships with young men they met in some casual situation. Dating followed. Soon they were in "steady" and exclusive relationships. In time, they surrendered to the young men's requests for sex because they felt they were loved, not because they were sexually passionate. These young women compromised a value and, in many cases, a virtue to secure loving devotion from their male friends.

Tearfully, they recounted how in a short time their boyfriends slowly withdrew their love. Dating was less frequent and their moments together were marked by conflicts. The good times were gone. When the young men began to date other girls, the relationships finally died from the lack of nurturing love. In tearful sessions these young women grieved and reproved themselves for not being lovely enough to keep the commitment of their boyfriends. But when they came to understand that they had been the prey of egocentric love, their anger surfaced.

Consider, also, the pain and disenchantment of the woman who falls in love with and marries a professional man who is a widower with children. Then discovers early in marriage that she is not her husband's lover, but has become only the mother of his children. He knew that he couldn't advance in his career if hampered by the demands of parenting. So he married a woman to fulfill these demands for him. His new wife performs the maternal role because she loves him and has even developed some love for the children. In exchange he gives only the love of his labors - financial provisions - not the gift of himself.

Her persistent demands for love and a closer relationship only drive him deeper into his work. And he is not particularly disturbed by her threats of divorce. He is confident that there will be another woman to replace her. And if he is lucky, she will be satisfied with homemaking and motherhood in exchange for financial security and social status. The relationship bonded in this way will then survive because both individuals will be using the same bond - egocentricity. Each will agree to be used as a means to the other's end.

Egocentric-love relationships are especially popular among gossip columnists. They feed on the misery of people whose lives are broken when their relationships crumble. Headlines a few years ago carried explicit accounts of Michael Tyson's emotional estrangement from his young wife, Robin Givens. Reportedly, she was carrying out her mother's plans to marry for money. While she claimed to be in love, reporters wrote that she had filed a $120 million law suit against Michael. How could he know if it was the loveliness of his person or the loveliness of his financial fortunes that attracted the interest of Ms. Givens? This question was concealed by the columnist's "objective" reporting of this "juicy" story. He concealed the question by reporting the seamy side of their lives.

Self-righteous moralists denounce the greed that leads people to marry for money. But even as they decry the avarice of these relationships, they secretly envy those who have the opportunity to pull it off. And so the younger woman of few means who marries the elderly wealthy man with no heirs is upbraided by envious observers for her greed and deceit. At the same time they covet the riches she will inherit. The love and honor she has pledged to the "old fool," as well as her daily loving and attending, are spurious. But the wealth it wins mollifies her conscience.

Many people, perhaps most, enter into marriage because they have needs they expect their spouses to fulfill. In addition to those who marry to attain wealth with its accompanying life of luxury, others hope to be rescued from an uncomfortable life condition. These include the husband who needs a mother for his children, the maltreated adolescent girl who needs a husband to escape from parental abuse, the alien who needs marriage to avoid deportation, the homosexual who needs a screen for his sexual inversion, and the rehabilitated criminal or drug addict who needs the strength and understanding of a loving spouse to keep from relapsing. In all of these situations, the need for a spouse is unmistakably clear.

There are other relationships, however, in which the need is less obvious. It is the need to be needed. Unable to feel that the person of the self merits love, a wife, for example, can earn love by fulfilling a need in her husband's life. And she enters into the marriage relationship unaware that it is her egocentricity that binds her to her husband.

If the dependent husband finds other ways to meet his need, the services of his helping wife are no longer required. The balance in their relationship is shifted. The wife, whose security in the relationship is now threatened, takes steps to restore that balance. The logical thing to do is create another dependency in him. She may do this by making suggestions, offering reminders, and giving instructions reprovingly. In this way, she demonstrates to him that he is inept and his life would be dreadful if it were not for her vigil. The message of his harassing wife is, "You can't get along without me."

Here are some situations that illustrate how the psychological interplay between the lack of self-love and selfless giving maintains relationships. It is not uncommon, for example, for a wife to become the breadwinner, as well as the homemaker and principal parent, because her husband refuses to secure employment. Or, the alcoholic husband maintains his lifestyle only because his wife faithfully compensates for his self-indulgence. Likewise, if a wife has a distaste for mothering and homemaking, choosing rather to be a social butterfly, her husband elects to assume more of these roles because he says, "I love my wife." These wives and husbands insist that they are still in love, not withstanding the irresponsible and unlovely behaviors they put up with. Even wives who have been treated harshly by their abusive husbands vow that they still love them. Without love for themselves, they suffer the indignities they feel their unloveliness deserves.

Egocentricity is present in the relationships of nearly all the couples who come to me for therapy. They have tried, however, to combine it with the bond of love. Unfortunately, they don't know where egocentricity ends and love begins. In the more seriously-troubled marriages, egocentricity has pushed love aside completely. It is here that I focus my treatment. If love for one another is still alive, I help spouses to rediscover it. I help them give it again the primacy and power to govern their relationships.

*   *   *

All crossed-bonded relationships leave in their aftermath disappointed and unhappy people. They last only as long as the involved parties tolerate their chronic frustration. These relationships, then, dissolve themselves.

The most painful personal and emotional injury that results from the dissolution of crossed-bonded relating occurs when one of the bonds is love. The remainder of this book, therefore, is devoted to love-bonded relationships, particularly as they relate to marriage.

PART III

Growing Out of Self and Growing in Love

For many years I stumbled along in marriage, busy working and earning degrees, certifications, and licenses and practicing simultaneously in religious, educational, and counseling psychology settings. With this career focus, I gave proportionately little to the growth of my love relationship with my wife. During our formative years of togetherness the marriage was solidly intact. The relationship, on the other hand, reached a plateau and moved along through the years solely on the strength of its own inertia - nothing lost, nothing added.

Now, looking at our relationship, I retrace the course that our lives have taken to bring it to its present level of richness and warmth that comes only from the mutual nurturing of a strong love-bond. I have learned that our love-bond has grown stronger because I have been able to make a greater contribution to it. My growth in giving to the relationship has followed the seldom traveled path that starts with self-love and ends in the heart and mind of another.

Like most children of the "Great Depression," I learned that individual worth was earned, not bestowed. One's worth was determined by what one produced for the good of the larger unit to which he or she belonged. This was particularly so in our

77

family of seven children whose mother died when the oldest child was 14, and whose father was largely an absentee member of the home.

Never unconditionally loved, I developed conditional self-love. I couldn't believe that I would be a lovely person without meeting the conditions that a *work ethic society* values - summed up in three words, *earn your love.*

In the remainder of this book I describe the path from growth in love for myself - thus releasing me from egocentric living - to the kindling of a new flame of love for my wife. I was not conscious of what was taking place, and it is only in retrospect that I have been able to construct the love map that led to this cherished goal. Using this map, over the years I have helped countless others on their spiritual pilgrimage to a sacred alliance of love in their relationships.

CHAPTER FIVE

The Challenge To Love

*love is at the top of the mountain and
you have to climb to reach it*

MARRIAGE WITHOUT LOVE

During one of our brief chats, a young counseling intern shared a portion of a conversation she had with a friend. Her friend had stated, "Well, after eight years, the romance has gone out of our relationship. I guess my husband and I will have to sit down and negotiate a new contract for our marriage." These remarks tell us much about the attitude of men and women who persevere in loveless marriages.

The loss of romance! I interpreted this to mean that they are finding no special pleasures in one another's company. Warm feelings are missing from their togetherness. Neither she nor her husband have the charm and beauty that once captured each other's hearts. They no longer see the loveliness in each other that blots out little faults and irritating habits. These are now annoyingly present. They don't experience sensations of "pins and needles" when they are touching, embracing, and kissing. Affectionate words and considerate acts of devoted caring don't have the power to be emotionally moving. Their minds have played out all of the fanciful images of love that earlier in their relationship created amorous feelings for each other. Gone are the compelling and passionate desires for sexual intimacies.

This young wife longed for the old love relationship, but felt it could not be recovered. She was willing to settle for an emotionally empty but harmonious marriage as a substitute for their lost love. Lovers can't restore an old romance. Nor, contrary to popular belief, should they try to revive it from its flickering embers when it has burned out. Romance is nothing more than a cataract that impairs the vision of the mind's eye - the only vision that recognizes true loveliness in another. (This theme is explored further in the chapter, *Igniting A New Flame*.)

"Love is blind," that is, the romanticism within which it is enshrouded doesn't allow the mind to see the person on whom it focuses. Still, millions of men and women follow its blindness in their search for a loving relationship and a happy marriage. They find and enjoy them for a little while. But with the waning of romance, they become confused by the diminished attraction they have for each other. For now they see clearly the "real" person that each is. They notice for the first time the flaws in one another's character, personality, and behavior. And with no romantic stirrings to bridle their tongues, their communication deteriorates into petty attacks on these newly discovered imperfections.

The "I" held in check by their romantic reveries now surges to the forefront. When they disagree, each hears from the other "I think...," "I need...," and "I wish..." Selflessness yields to self-centeredness, parading itself in actions and words that promote, please, and, yes, pamper the self. They have replaced the bond of love in the relationship with the bond of egocentricity, which takes firm control of their interactions.

When we take a closer look at romantic love, we discover that much of its incentive is the self-indulging demands of the giver. Listening to unhappy couples express the frustration they experience in their relationships, I hear disappointing sighs following graphic descriptions of the emotional exhilaration of affectionate togetherness they once shared. I hear fond recollections of passionate arousal they felt when being touched and held. And I hear forthright complaints that "she doesn't turn me on any more." These messages tell me that romantics are concerned more about the feelings they receive from their loving than those they create for their beloved.

With the languishing of a romantic high comes the loss of loving attentiveness to the person by whom it was aroused. And if that person is still "in love," the relationship easily becomes a battle of conflicting perceptions of what has gone wrong.

Many men and women don't question why they aren't successful in love until they have had a series of relationship failures. One of my patients - a middle-aged male business executive in his third marriage and carrying on a clandestine extramarital affair - acknowledged that his philandering would stop only when he came to understand the "need" in his life that he expected women to fulfill. Weary of his fickleness, he said, "This running after women has to stop. You have to help me figure out what it is about them that I need. I'm tired of getting myself into one relationship after another and hurting a lot of people in the process."

Focusing the therapy on his current affair, I asked what he found so appealing about his paramour. He replied honestly and directly, "I feel relaxed when I'm with her. And I enjoy discussing things with her. She is willing to listen to what I have to say. She understands what I'm thinking or feeling without asking me, and doesn't interrupt me when I'm talking. I just feel good when I'm with her." Note that his response is punctuated with eight references to himself. And, although he did not mention them in his answer, he alluded on other occasions to the pleasant "love making" sessions, which he enjoyed with unrestrained sensuousness. During these periods of sexual relating he was lifted in passion from his cheerless life. Here, too, the "I" was the controlling force in the relationship.

Essentially, he had described the rapture of romance. He placed himself in the center of this woman's life when they were together. He took from their relationship what he needed and gave only what he chose to give. She, in turn, didn't ask him to help her carry any of the burdens of her personal life. Most importantly, while enjoying the "fruits" of their relationship, he ignored her less admirable traits. In a nutshell, he had said to me, "I enjoy all the excitement and fascination of love in a warm and emotional aura without committing myself beyond our romantic rendezvous."

When asked how this relationship differed from the relationships with his former wives and his current spouse, during the early stages of courtships, he admitted that there was little difference. He received from them the same personal satisfactions and emotional feelings he was obtaining from his present "love." Each affair provided a romantic narcosis during which he had no conscious and discerning awareness of the real woman with whom he had fallen in love. He found that in the cuddling comfort of his lovers' arms the darkness in his life became bright and his despair turned to joy.

Romantic love is deceptive. It appears to be totally vested in the other person. A man and woman caught in the *trance* of romantic love believe that it is one another's spellbinding loveliness that captures their "love." What they can't see is that their love affair is really an obsession with romantic ecstasy. The quest for an endless high binds them together, not their loveliness.

Come Into My Life

Lovers drawn to each other by the magnetic pull of an addictive romance are bonded almost exclusively by egocentricity. They need each other in order to experience their highs. Romantics aren't aware that their motives are self-serving. Because the high is so intensely pleasurable, they meet to secure their "fix." And, since each receives equally, each gives equally.

When a lover, the man for example, ceases to be passionately inflamed by the woman he has loved, he gives less time to the relationship and loves with less ardor. He stops giving devoted attentiveness to his former beloved from whom the high cannot now be obtained. The forsaken lover, however, still yearns for the highs. She gives even more time, more attention, and more of self to restore the romantic bond. She will give, do, and be whatever is necessary to prolong the romance of the relationship. If, however, she fails to revive his romantic commitment, her own love turns to wrath.

Shirley and Phil

I have found that many times a rejected lover is not in a position to vent her vengeance against the partner whose romantic flame has burned out. So she lashes out at those who sincerely love her. The relationship of Shirley and Phil is a case in point. Both were in their late thirties, married for more than ten years, and parents of small children. When Phil came to me for help, he launched immediately into a long and detailed description of an affair his wife was having. The romance within that affair, however, had peaked. Her lover, also married and a father, had come down from his romantic high. His perceptions of Shirley and his vision of the entire relationship had become much sharper. His love had faded, and his withdrawal left Shirley emotionally crestfallen.

Alone with her grief, Shirley's anger spilled all over those closest to her. She turned against her husband and blamed him for her infidelity. In her periodic tirades she methodically shredded his "ego" with a litany of complaints. She maliciously blamed him for all her unhappiness, placing no curbs on her vitriolic attacks. "You make my skin crawl; sex was never any good with you; I just faked and pretended; you never met my emotional needs; because of you my life has been meaningless; I have never had a moment of joy with you; I feel dead and empty: you drove me to this affair."

As Phil related these stinging pronouncements to me, his voice quivered and tears welled in his eyes. His pain was evident as he tried to describe the depth to which his spirits had plummeted, "I am totally devastated. My home is breaking up; my whole future is gone." In his pleadings he had said to her, "This is all fantasy stuff, just idealizations. Having a little cabin in the woods where you can kick off your shoes is not real."

Even her parents came under attack. Shirley told them how tortured she felt living with Phil and how much she really loved her paramour. They, in turn, called me, hoping to get some understanding of their daughter's behavior. They believed that Phil had been a faithful and affectionate husband. Her mother could only conclude that Shirley "had flipped her lid."

Robert F. Forman, drawing from Stanton Peele's book, *Love and Addiction*, has written an intriguing treatise in which he views a romantic high as lovesickness and compares it to an addiction. Forman examines the symptoms beginning with the craving and obsession and concludes with the withdrawal and recovery, and in many cases the relapse. Citing Peele, he wrote "...people's love relations can look an awful lot like addiction. The opposite, however, is equally true. People's addictions can look an awful lot like love."[1] The symptoms, he notes, parallel those of individuals suffering with drug or alcohol addiction.

Although lovesickness is common with adolescents, it can occur at any age. Like drug addicts, "romantic junkies" surrender to their addiction, losing control over thoughts, judgements, and feelings. Their lives become unmanageable. Still, they pursue the addictive life style. They can't acknowledge the significant pain they are suffering, and causing others to suffer. Nor can they think about the emotional anguish and tormenting disillusionment that lies at the end of their thoughtless extravagance.

We can't have happy personal, emotional, and sexual relationships when we become the object of our own love. More importantly, when we dote upon ourselves we can't know the richness of a genuinely contented life.

The efforts of romantics to attract loving admiration from others is circular. They pursue love, win it, bask in it briefly, become bored with it, abandon it, and set out to find a new love. Except for that brief period of time in which they enjoy their victories, they continue to be filled with an undefined loneliness and the painful annoyance of unfulfilled love. But as narcissists, they have no strong feelings of sadness, nor do they grieve their loss. It's simply on to the next conquest. They are never emotionally quieted.

We can't close our eyes to the narcissistic character of a romantic relationship simply because it offends us to think of it that way. It is exploitative, and the lovers have no substantive or sustained respect for one another.

And like all other aspects of self-centered loving, the sexual embrace is only a self-serving pleasure, not an expression of love. Sexual excitement serves only to intensify the illusion of loveliness which narcissistic lovers think they see in each other. But it is only the final step in the conquest, the most glowing moment of the relationship that precedes the ebbing of the romantic high. Following sexual intimacies, idealizations begin to weaken, foretelling the end of the relationship. The lover, whose fantasy of ideal love has crumbled, emerges from the relationship confused and disillusioned. The idealized person who has been callously cast aside comes out of it both confused and deeply hurt.

All of us long to be loved. It is a human psychological and spiritual need. "I was looking for love out there," said a young adult male who was dying from AIDS. He was responding to his television host who had asked why he had not taken seriously the risk associated with indiscriminate homosexual behavior. His answer shows his desperate craving. He accepted the peril of his behavior because his need for relief from his loneliness, coupled with an emotional hunger, was greater than his fear of dying.

Because our need to be loved and to belong are so psychologically and emotionally strong, we follow one of many different paths to fulfill them. We shape our lives in the mold of others to be approved and accepted by them. We adopt group values as the condition for becoming one of its members. By climbing the ladder of success we gain esteem from those less successful. If fortunate enough to achieve high status, we exercise its power to command attention and deference. With the accumulation of wealth, we attract those who covet it. Individuals with less integrity resort to deception, charm, promises, dependency, and sexual seduction. They all arrive at the same end, disillusioned, disappointed, and still seeking personal fulfillment in a love relationship.

In an interview with Otto Kernberg, Linda Wolfe queried, "You are suggesting that it is a given that in order to feel fulfilled as human beings, we must feel deeply for others, whether our society promotes attachment or urges us away from it." His response: "Yes, I think so. All other things being equal, there is something that happens to one in a deep relationship with someone else which brings great satisfaction to the individual. It has been called *transcendence*, the sense of extending beyond oneself and feeling a sense of unity with all others who have lived and loved and suffered - whether it is one's parents or people throughout history. And when this can't be attained, one feels emptiness and chronic dissatisfaction."[2]

Most couples who come to me for marriage counseling have never known this sense of "transcendence." They have never developed a deep relationship with another person because their love has been trapped within themselves. Engrossed in their quest for love, they haven't searched for the loveliness in each other. Without this discernment of loveliness there is no bond across which devoted love can pass from themselves to the other. Their lives are empty. They live in a state of chronic hunger because they feast on a narcissistic love that can never satisfy them.

The human soul, the spiritual seat of our being, cannot experience that sense of oneness with another person through machine-like verbal and behavioral networking of our physical lives, regardless of how harmoniously it is done. It is a cruel hoax for marriage counselors to lead couples to believe that they can find happiness and emotional fulfillment by helping them to manage their relationships mechanically and tactfully. This approach suggests that they can live in the center of themselves and still love one another if they are thoughtful, discreet, and exercise good judgement.

Helping spouses to learn the art of communication is basic to marriage counseling. Counselors teach listening and how to observe and interpret non-verbal cues - silence, facial expressions, gestures, body posture, and voice tones. They give rules for arguing or, as some call it, "how to fight fair." Clients learn the art of skillfully disagreeing without malice. Counselors show them how to define a problem and how to attack it without personally assaulting one other.

As I work with them, I get the impression that counselors view marriage as a kind of game. Husbands and wives are the contestants and victory - harmony in relating - is achieved through good sportsmanship. And sportsmanship results from proficiency in communication skills that are developed from rigorous practice. As long as each follows the rules and doesn't allow verbal and behavioral interactions to get outside of their rational control, the relationship goes on.

However, experience has taught me that over time, our "cognitive watchdog" grows weary of guarding against making mechanical blunders. It then yields to the selfishness of our needs, desires, and feelings. They take control again. Egocentricity asserts itself anew, setting in motion a new round of conflicts.

Although couples don't mention it, in most instances because they can't identify what it is, there is something missing from their lives when they come out of marriage counseling with nothing more than a peaceful coexistence. That something is a "transcendent" union. In its place is a feeling of emptiness, a void which they expected would be filled by one another's flow of nurturing love.

Most couples complete long-term marriage counseling with considerably less than they expected to receive. They relate compatibly, and have the tools and skills to resolve personal conflicts. And in some measure they have gained control of their feelings. But they have not achieved a deep awareness of one another's loveliness. And without this, they retain inner directed relating. They fail to learn that they cannot keep love in the center of themselves and at the same time be personally, spiritually, and emotionally filled.

THE CHALLENGE

Love Relationship therapists who challenge men and women to build their marriages on the foundation of love need to know the strength of the forces against which they contend. To stop loving the self and learn to love another is a formidable challenge.

> *I need to depart from my text here and distinguish between the "love for self" and "being in love with self." The first is affectionate self-regard, but other directed. The second is narcissistic ego-fixation and self directed.*

I got my first real insight into this challenge when I began to study the lifestyle of the young people who exploded on the social scene of the 1960's - a style characterized by a consuming preoccupation with self-indulgence. Beginning in the late fifties, it burst into full bloom during the following two decades. Its hold on their lives was never broken.

I had just accepted my current university appointment, and one of my first assignments was to teach "The Psychology of the Adolescent" to graduate level students. I knew I could not teach this course effectively without understanding the causes of the revolt among young people that was taking place from one end of the country to the other.

Surveying the literature, I came across an essay written by John W. Aldridge, titled "In the Country of the Young."[3] Aldridge argues that the Great Depression and World War II led to the takeover of this country by its young people. These two events, he contends, conditioned their parents to think of themselves as a "sacrificial generation."[4] Having wearily survived back-to-back traumas, with their lasting psychic effects, these parents were grateful simply for life's necessities.

The children rushed in to fill the void that these traumas created for their parents. And the parents cooperated fully by allowing them to dictate the terms of relating with them. They found themselves busy taking their children "to" and bringing them "from," playing with them, buying for them, and worrying about them. No plans were made without first considering the children.

Rather than being appreciative for the sacrifice and the love they received, the young became contemptuous of their parents, convinced that they were "...dead all along and only they (the children) were alive."[5] It was, after all, reasonable for them to conclude that they must be very special people to receive such generosity. With little respect for their parents, they developed a grossly inflated admiration for themselves.

Come Into My Life

Then, when their children failed to show affectionate appreciation, parents catered even more to their every demand - money, cars, clothes, music records - for their "endlessly diversionary existence."[6] The final result says Aldridge: "...life in America became frozen - apparently for good - at the level of utilitarian existence."[7]

This generation grew up, he asserts, perceiving itself as a "herd." And so collectively they set out to save the world. They professed love for the masses whom they did not know. If they had known, says Aldridge, they probably would have withheld their love from them. It was "...a generation which seemed never to have been alone; hence they had never endured psychological isolation or been compelled to develop the perspective of otherness."[8]

Without a strong and active *intrapersonal* relationship, individuals cannot develop self-identities. And without self-identity, they can't develop an awareness of the distinct identities of other people.

The generation of the sixties didn't have, what Aldridge terms, the "spectatorial attitude"[9] that focuses on the lives of other people. Without that focus they could not see in others their beauty and ugliness, strengths and weaknesses, positive and negative qualities, and their needs and desires. Looking at others they saw only how they could use them to serve their own ends.

They struggled for the preservation of the herd from which their needs were met. They, as individuals, were the end of all their striving; the group was the means. Thus, Aldridge concludes, came a generation of adults with a single personality - bland, selfish, impatient, and tolerant only of those who were like themselves.

It is primarily this generation of married couples that marriage counselors are called to serve. With few exceptions, we can say that marriages have broken down because husbands and wives expect each other to fulfill their self-centered demands, as did their parents who gave birth to and nurtured their egocentricity. They react instantly with displeasure when their wants are ignored. And they become defensively angry if accused of thoughtlessly failing to fulfill each other's desires. Nearly every couple entering counseling begins with each spouse attacking the other for being a washout in the marriage.

It is against this backdrop that I challenge husbands and wives to love each other. Whether Aldridge is correct in his explanation of the etiology of the egocentricity that has shaped life in our society for the last thirty years is not important. But it is important that we acknowledge that men and women, during these three decades, have taken with them into their marriages self-indulging expectations they refuse to relinquish.

My task is to help spouses dislodge themselves from the center of their lives in order that the other may enter in. If it is not the quest for an insatiable romantic high or the conditioning of 25 or more years of indulgence - first by parents and then by the individuals themselves - it is specific psychological needs of one or both partners that must be hurdled before they can give up their self-indulgence.[10] But any one, or any combination of two or all three of these conditions, may be the obstacle standing in the way of a husband's or wife's attempt to give love to the other. Whichever hurdle it is, I always encounter strong resistance when I challenge them to overcome it and give each other the love they have been giving themselves.

During the early seventies I evoked angry rebuttals from graduate students when I introduced Aldridge's article for their consideration. They were convinced that all prior generations had suffered because they were stifled by the repressive environment in which they were forced to live. Borrowing their arguments from the *progressive* counseling theorists whose works were spawned by the liberal movement, they assailed Aldridge's position. They defended their convictions with such shopworn phrases as "self-awareness," "self-fulfillment," "personal growth," and "self-actualization." So with this movement came the proliferation of individual and group counseling theories which these young graduate students eagerly embraced as their favorite treatment models to help others reach the lofty peak of *highest self.*

Over the last fifteen years I have taught a course in counseling theories to more than six hundred graduate students. They are now the counselors who help couples whose marriages and families are falling apart. They are well received because they don't expect their clients to give up their self-absorbing lives. Instead, they teach them when and how to discreetly practice *some* self-denial, how to cognitively manage their communication, and how to amicably negotiate conflicts. When they end counseling, their clients may have achieved marital harmony but deep inside they yearn for something more. That something is love. But they can never have it because their "marital technicians" have not challenged them to love one another.

The case of Phil and Shirley, cited earlier, illustrates this point. Phil told me that his wife had been asked by a counselor if she had counseling in the past. She said, "Yes, we were in counseling with Dr. Zimmerman." Her response was, "Bad choice! Bad choice! He always tries to keep couples together when they're not satisfied with their relationships. You have a right to the romantic feelings you say you're not receiving from

93

your marriage." When this wife and mother mentioned the pain and hardship that divorce would bring, her counselor simply replied, "Someone has to wear the black hat."

Returning to her husband, she used the counselor's advocacy to justify her behavior and absolve her of blame. This counselor, married and divorced several times, unfortunately seems to have dispensed the same advice she used to work through her own relationships.

I took personal comfort that she singled me out as a therapist who tries to help couples preserve their marriages. I attempt to do so by helping them convert their professions of love into actions of love. Beginning with whatever amount of love they have for one another, I help them shed their self-indulgence so they can release that love and give it to the other. But when both, or frequently one partner only, disavows any love for the other, I can't put love into their hearts and minds. I can only show them how to give life to the love they already have.

THE CHANGE PROCESS

Initially, I work with husbands and wives individually. My goal is to assist each spouse to remove the self from the center of his and her life. I see them separately for two reasons. First, the development of "love-bonding" hinges on the elimination of the divisiveness of egocentricity that each brings to the relationship. So reconciliation in the initial stage of therapy is not a primary consideration. Secondly, they have a right to confidentially disclose their emotionally painful, personally embarrassing, and embedded-in feelings of failure and guilt without baring their private selves to their mates.

Come Into My Life

I expect each spouse to accept personal responsibility for dethroning the self. This begins with the reframing of the self-concept. We live from the center of ourselves because we lack self-love. Kernberg asserts in his writings that self-hatred, not self-love, is the driving force underlying narcissism. To the extent that we demand attention from others, insist upon having our own way, expect to be unconditionally accepted and loved, are blinded to our own faults, magnify the flaws in others, and cannot sense the hurt we cause for others, then it is to this extent we hold ourselves in self-contempt. We use these narcissistic behaviors to hide our self-loathing feelings from others, as well as from ourselves. So I help husbands and wives develop love for themselves. Only then can they be set free from their narcissism and be able to center their love in one another.

Young people of the sixties and seventies did not love. They did not love the establishment that frustrated and refused to pamper them. They did not love their parents who were wimpish and refused to be adversaries with whom they could battle and thus find their adulthood. They did not love their country, burning its flag in their crusade for "world brotherhood." They did not love the unborn, aborting their fetuses because, as children, they had no time for child-rearing. They did not love one another. They freely used each other for their own ends and to be collectively strong enough to fight against any and all who opposed their self-indulgence. They did not love themselves, choosing to waste their lives with drugs and alcohol, to degrade themselves with sexual debauchery, and to end their lives intentionally with suicide.

These young insurgents are the men and women who, now many years later, are struggling with their marriages. They struggle because they cannot love. They cannot love because they have no love to give. And they have no love to give because they do not perceive themselves as lovely, and only loveliness begets love.

In their earlier developmental years they lived to please themselves. There were no absolutes to guide behaviors and relationships. Right and wrong, good and bad were determined by the pleasure or satisfaction which they obtained from their behaviors. They demanded the right to assert their menacing individuality with little consideration for others. Their message was clear, "Accept me as I am, or don't accept me at all."

This generation of young people discovered how to form "love" relationships and at the same time retain commitment to self. If one person became possessive and demanding, the relationship was terminated. The two individuals would simply drift into other relationships and remain with new partners until they had again worn out their usefulness to each other. They saw nothing demeaning in "using" others or in "being used" by them for self-gratification. Egocentricity was free to run its course with no curbs on its desires, and with no responsibility for the welfare of others.

Spoiled children have no beauty. Their greed causes other children to shun them. Their teachers or adult supervisors see them as inconsiderate little brats. They are without social or personal charm, and any friendliness they display is a ploy to lure other children and adults into their servitude.

In adults, these behaviors are just as blatantly apparent. The spoiled child within them rebels by crying, sulking, or screaming when their demands are ignored. And so they censure and verbally abuse one another when their insistence for indulgence is denied or thwarted.

Here are some of the many complaints that spouses voice about one another in therapy with me. They illustrate the ways in which they serve themselves in their marriages.

WIVES' COMPLAINTS

When we come home from work he just turns on the TV, while I have to pick up the kids and prepare dinner.

All he does is work, and when he does have time off he goes golfing with the guys.

We only have sex when he wants it, and then it's over in a couple of minutes.

He stops after work and has supper with his mother and doesn't tell me; I have a complete meal ready and have to eat alone.

When we go out he spends more time talking to other men's wives than he does with me.

He just takes me for granted, never consults me about anything we are going to do.

He's always putting me down in front of company and makes me the brunt of his jokes and smart remarks.

He complains all the time; he's too meticulous about everything.

He doesn't like to be around people; he's a loner and always absorbed in himself.

I want some affection, and he never touches me unless we're having sex.

He controls and dominates everything.

His life has no variety and excitement.

He looks at me in terms of ownership; I'm his property.

He compares me to his mother as a houseworker; the house is never clean enough.

He thinks I should be nothing but a career housewife, and that turns me off.

I have been married to him for 17 years, and he was never committed to the relationship.

He intimidates me.

He is never complimentary and loving.

He will never do anything for me, even when I ask him.

He can never say, "I love you."

He flirts with other women in front of me.

He is like a child tugging at my skirt.

The only reason he loves me is for what I do for him, the home, and the kids.

He never picks up after himself.

He wants a nice home but doesn't want to work at it.

HUSBANDS' COMPLAINTS

My wife always blames me for everything.

She is too dependent and expects me to carry all the responsibilities of the home.

She spends all our money on clothes.

She is never honest with me; I never know her true feelings.

My wife brings her bad mood to the family dinner, and I don't know how to deal with it.

I have to tiptoe around her just to keep peace.

She's rigid; everything is right or wrong; there is no gray.

If she could be happier, I would be closer and more pleasant.

She is critical and catastrophizes everything.

She keeps threatening to break up the marriage just to make me angry.

Come Into My Life

My wife sees everything negative; she looks up and sees the clouds and never the sun; it's my job to brighten the day.

She takes every little discussion into an argument.

She professes to roll with the punches, yet is compulsive about everything.

She avoids me all day and then goes to bed and wants to be cuddled.

She likes the fast life and wants to be with the "shakers and movers."

She runs the home like a general manager.

All she ever talks about is the house and material things.

I told her I didn't need a mother; I already have one.

I have listened to her whining for two years, and I am getting tired of it.

I am always giving, and I would like to get something back.

She married me only for security; she needs someone to lean on; I don't feel loved.

She has to be with me all the time. I feel tied down.

She is always cutting me up.

She tries to break my spirit.

I'm always getting long lectures.

I never do anything right; I feel like one of her second graders.

She out-talks me all the time.

I don't know what she wants me to be, I guess a knight in shining armor.

She hides her softness and emotions.

I want to make it clear that there is certainly nothing lovely about any of these behaviors. But, this is the key to understanding how people bind themselves to one another. The bond of love, used initially during courtship to win a mutual commitment, has been replaced by egocentric bindings. With these bondings securely in place, they now steadfastly refuse to be forced from the center of their lives. And they show only the minimum level of loveliness needed to keep the relationship together. As long as they unconditionally accept one another, even with some friction, there will be no change in their behaviors. When the friction reaches a level of chronic painful tolerance for one or both spouses, then they reach out for counseling.

Marriage counselors who use a management approach to counseling begin by facilitating a change in behaviors to restore harmony. Compromises and concessions are negotiated without awakening sensitivities and compassion. The goal of their counseling is marital reconciliation. If they are successful, their clients will have togetherness without tenderness, communication without feeling, and sex without love. They will have what they felt they needed, but they will still be longing for what they really wanted - to be desired and loved.

They do not receive love because in most instances they have not requested it. In the beginning of therapy when I ask a wife, for example, why she objects to a particular behavior her husband regularly exhibits, I receive a variety of evasive answers: "It's not fair...A husband shouldn't treat his wife this way... It's hurting our marriage...I'm getting tired of it." All of these things may be true, but the pain from which she wants release lies much deeper. Hoping to get in touch with that pain I offer in a tender way the truthful answer I believe she would like to give to me: "You're feeling very hurt, aren't you? You would like him to love you and to show his love by his actions. His lack of consideration makes you feel like you aren't sweet enough or good enough to be loved by him." Bowing her head, with tears and in a halting voice, she replies, "Yeah, I guess."

These few statements from me change the entire tone of our session. The focus shifts from her husband to herself. Her bitterness and resentment lose their force, surrendering to a pensive and meditative mood. Her eyes no longer project anger. They now evoke my empathy.

At this point, counseling changes to therapy, i.e., from a discussion of problems to the healing of a heart. Now comes an honest recognition of the failure of the marriage. It is floundering because it has deteriorated into a contest in which they, like two children, are vying for a position in the center of the relationship. The unity they may once have had is gone. They have replaced love for one another with the re-establishment of self-indulgence.

With a wounded heart plainly visible, it is clear what the healing process requires. Each must give love for the other the position and prominence that their self again occupies. We put problems and conflicts on hold while we set out to achieve this goal.

When individuals do not love themselves, they seek confirmation of loveliness from an external source. Spouses become the reasonable choices to provide that confirmation.

It's usually necessary as therapy progresses to uncover the origin of their failure to become self-loving. In nearly all cases I find that they demand the unconditional love they received, or failed to receive, from their parents. They expect each other to become what I term a "parentified spouse." Their disputes reflect anger and resentment towards one another for failing to fulfill this parental role. The fault is not in their failures to perform the role, but in their expectations. They fully anticipate receiving unconditional love as an entitlement of marital bonding. Adults, even in marriage, do not give unconditional love in the same continuing manner as parents give to their children. If it has not been received in childhood, it is forever lost.

Love is attracted only to loveliness. I help husbands and wives look at themselves and make some determination about their loveliness. Together we probe into their behaviors, communications, and attitudes. We determine how lovely they are by how they please or offend their spouses.

This probing is emotionally painful. To ease the pain, spouses use every opportunity to redirect the blame. It's always easier to point to the unloveliness in another than to acknowledge it in oneself. So it is common for them to inject a defensive statement such as, "Yes, but she is more...than I am." The thrust of therapy is to assist them to develop loveliness, and this cannot be done until their unloveliness is exposed, pain not withstanding.

I have said repeatedly that we can't love another without first loving self. And we love the self only when we perceive it as loveable. Personal traits, actions, manners of speech, moods, and attitudes are the media though which we communicate our beauty.

When our emotional and personal dispositions become repugnant to us, generally we direct our self-rejection outwardly against others. In this way we deny self-awareness of our shortcomings and character blemishes - in short, our unloveliness. Lacking this awareness, we have no inducement for change. And so we continue, fruitlessly, to expect affectionate devotion with no loveliness to attract it.

Come Into My Life

I teach my patients self-love by helping them to accept all that is attractive in their lives and eliminate the unattractive. The unattractive qualities must go. They have no place in the life of a lovely person. They can no more love these qualities in themselves than they can love them in their spouses.

They discover quickly how difficult it is to shed unlovely behaviors and habits. They persist because they are intrinsic to, and inseparable from, the selfishness which controls their lives.

Selfishness has no beauty. So they can't achieve self-love until they become unselfish - living with the center of life outside of self. Free from the constraints of self-seeking, they can then search for the loveliness in one another and commit themselves in love to it. And by loving, they lay back the folds of an even deeper beauty, and their attractiveness becomes more inviting.

The most gratifying reward I receive from doing love relationship therapy is sharing in the growth of each spouse's self-respect and self-admiration. This growth releases them from self, and they reach out to one another. Their lives take on a deeper meaning and a new kind of pride. They know, perhaps for the first time, the joy of making another person truly happy.

Loving the self, they need less confirming adoration and attention from one another. Each feels a sense of wholeness, depending less upon the other for completion of the self. They are pleased to be able to give themselves to each other as a total and self-affirming person. This is their true gift of love.

Anxiety diminishes as they are released from the grasp of self-centered love and its endless, selfish demands. I see healing of the spirit and mind of a man and a woman whose lives were empty, and who wept inside over pain they could not identify.

Other more tangible indications of the increasing acceptance and love of self do not escape my attention. I listen as they

103

gradually shift from "issues" in the relationship to the "you and me" within the relationship. And in a cheerful and comfortable way they examine their relationship bond to determine the extent to which it is being formed from the loveliness each is contributing to it. Having become comfortable with the probing analysis of their personalities and behaviors, they are no longer defensive and evasive. When unloveliness is pointed out, they take ownership of it and initiate the changes that comply more with the requirements of love.

Accusations and complaints decrease because love, unlike a frail ego, isn't so sensitive to emotional or personal assaults. Objections to behaviors become tender requests for change, not retaliatory attempts to place blame. Because the language of love is *intuitively* acquired, they achieve changes in their communication without deliberately structuring their verbal exchanges.

They have a growing patience with the manner in which I am providing assistance to them. When therapy is initiated, one or both spouses is anxious and feels a sense of urgency. However, as we progress towards the establishment of love as the foundation of their relationship, and the key to conflict resolution, a sense of serenity permeates the therapy hour. When a husband or wife enters my office and asks me, "How are you?" I know, then, that they are less anxious and more comfortable with the pace of the therapeutic movement.

They look forward to receiving direction and support for their growth in love. By living their professions of love for each other, I know they have cognitively and emotionally ingested the precepts that I have helped them to learn.

CHAPTER SIX

Love Of Me
Before Love Of You

there can be no love for another without love for self

If we live by the teachings of the Christian faith, we are commanded to "...love your neighbor as you love yourself."[1] Interestingly, the command to "...love your neighbor..." does not stand alone. It is accompanied by the phrase, "as you love yourself." Does this mean that because we are human, we are to be loved equally by self and by others? If so, the moral force behind the command is the equal and common good of humankind. This is one interpretation of this text.

Most people, however, interpret it simply as a straightforward, sacred tenet to be accepted literally and applied universally. Because a sovereign God gave this teaching, we should not question its rule for our lives. It needs no interpretation. If we accept the command literally it then becomes *immoral* not to love self, as well as not to love others. It is honorable then, and even expected, that we should love ourselves. We must be careful, therefore, not to become so concerned with the morality of loving others that we overlook the directive that to "love yourself" is just as morally binding. Self-love is neither a sin

105

nor a personal flaw in character, when it is balanced with equal love for other people.

These two interpretations differ only in terms of the authority behind the injunction, human compassion or divine decree. We need to accept both to completely understand this command. But understanding is not our failure. We acknowledge that all of our problems are caused by excluding love from our relationships. The question is, "Why can't we, then, obey the *divine* instruction to show *human* compassion?"

Social scientists, and religious leaders alike, have been unable to answer this question. They cannot help us because they use only one-half of the command, "you shall love your neighbor," in formulating their answers. They focus on the evil of not loving others and ignore the immorality of not loving self. To love self is a sacred mandate that is not given the attention that it is meant to have.

There can be no increase in love for others until there is growing love for self. It is not possible for me to love another if I have only contempt for myself. If I believe that I am an unlovely person, I reasonably conclude that others will scoff at my offerings of love. The disturbing question that prompts me to keep my love to myself is, "Who would want any love from me?" So, fearing rejection, I withhold my love.

At the other extreme is the person who has much love for self and also much love for others. This individual readily and liberally gives when love is called for. The love that is shared is worthy because the *source from which it flows is worthy*. No thought is given to rejection. And if the love were to be refused, the giver would not attribute the refusal to the lack of his or her personal loveliness. So, if we want people to love more, and not fear rejection, we must first help them grow in love for themselves.

106

Come Into My Life

Self-love is not to be confused with self-indulgence or self-devotion. These traits are uncomplimentary because they wrap people up in their own lives. They cannot see either the needs or the loveliness of others that evoke compassion and love.

Love of self, in the context about which I speak, is both positive and commendable. People who have a wholesome love for themselves genuinely appreciate their personal goodness. They value themselves as deserving human beings. Because they love themselves, they don't accept malicious treatment from those who wrongfully abuse them. They recognize their personal weaknesses but do not vilify the *whole of self* when only a *part of self* needs purging. They are self-confirming, even when censured by others. If a self-loving person says, "I love me," we are not offended by his candor. It is not arrogance or an ego out of control that speaks. It is an expression of worth acknowledged and properly ascribed to self.

Loving self before trying to love others is a principle that marriage counselors do not include in their practice. Rather, they attempt to help their clients change their behaviors and thereby relate more compatibly. They do this by appealing to their sense of responsibility and to the logic of making reasonable concessions, all to achieve the goal of getting along in marriage.

In love relationship therapy I want my clients to achieve more than marital compatibility. I want them to feel more complete within themselves, and better able to choose their behaviors rather than be controlled by them. Here is where I begin therapy, with the self-concept of each spouse.

If a wife, for example, has very little love for herself, she will adopt one of several behavioral styles to compensate for her feelings of unloveliness. Unable to feel worth in herself, she may attempt to obtain it from a marriage to a "worthy" man.

107

She avoids rejection from her husband by shaping her life to become pleasing and acceptable to him. Her forfeiture of self may even reach a point in which the husband lives life for both of them. The wife, in this instance, says through her behavior, "Your interests are my interests; your meaning for life is my meaning for life; your values are my values; your wishes are my wishes, and your hopes are my hopes. In fact, *your being is my being*." The wife hereby discredits herself and attempts to merge with her husband to acquire worthiness that she feels she otherwise can never achieve. I can best illustrate these various adaptive and compensatory styles of relating by sharing some examples from my files.

Carol and Rob

Carol married Rob, a man whom she perceived to be industrious and responsible, destined to become successful in his career. Through the years, Rob changed employment many times. Changes always meant moving, often great distances. Ultimately he rose to the level of vice president in his company's hierarchy of management. His climb had consumed long hours and years of devoted time. His diligence and dedication to work enabled him to achieve his goal. But the struggle depleted his energy and spirit. Tired and weary most of the time, he invested little of himself in the home and family. Carol assumed the major role of homemaking and the parenting of their children. Dutifully, in each community in which the family settled, she enrolled the children in school, became the liaison between the home and the childrens' social groups, and was the troubleshooting parent when the children acted mischievously or experienced learning problems in school. She meticulously decorated each house into which the family moved, choosing colors and styles to create an atmosphere of comfort and warmth. Carol and the children accepted the disruptions of their lives when Rob's schedule conflicted with their plans and activities. She subscribed largely to Rob's life meanings and values. He was the worthier person. He would bring success and happiness to both their lives.

When she called me for an appointment, Carol was 53 years old, with a diffused self and feeling personally empty and unfulfilled. She was emotionally estranged from her husband who was still invested in himself through his work. Most disappointing of all, Carol never gained the worth she had hoped to achieve through her husband's career success. Adding to her troubled spirit was the feeling of failure as a parent. Her children were personally and vocationally floundering in their adult lives.

Because she could not love herself, she took the role of a servant to her husband. She believed that in this way she was showing love for him. In the beginning of the relationship, without awareness, she had concluded that she was marrying a person who was more important then herself. Almost by design, Carol lost herself in the ongoing life of her husband. While attempting to *use* him as a *means* to her personal elevation, she became more deeply mired in her feelings of low self-esteem. Her self-love was diminished, not enlarged.

Bruce and Dee

Other relationships evolve in which one person - again it is usually the woman - not only becomes a servant but surrenders to mental and, sometimes, physical abuse. The self is so devalued that she actually feels she merits her husband's abuse. This was the situation I confronted in the relationship between Dee and Bruce. It was Bruce who called for therapy. When his call came, he was living with another woman, an employee of a large business firm which he managed. In our first session he said, "I can't decide if I want to divorce and marry my girlfriend or go back to my wife." While he wrestled with this decision, Dee was at home caring for their teenage children and waiting, hoping, and willing to accept him back. Bruce frequently voiced guilt about the mental anguish and emotional pain he caused for Dee. But his words lacked feelings of genuine remorse.

As therapy progressed Dee became deeply involved in the process of healing their broken relationship. In our sessions I plunged with her to the depth of pain she was experiencing from the emotional wounds inflicted by Bruce's self-indulging and calloused behavior. In the course of treatment, which continued for more than a year in both individual and couple sessions, Bruce left the home twice only to return two or three weeks later. When he was prepared to leave for a third time, his supervisor assigned him to a branch of the firm in a distant city. I continued to see him and Dee on an irregular basis for several weeks following the move. As of this writing, I have learned that they have been living together for the last several years.

Dee wanted to believe that her devotion to Bruce sprang from a sincere love for him. But, as I saw it, she was taken in by her own self-deception. What she thought to be love for Bruce was admiration for his business success and status. Acceptance of this insight did not come easily for her.

Throughout the many long hours of treatment she insisted that, "This is just a middle-age fling that will soon be over, and he will be home to stay." Yet, there were times when she talked about divorcing him. And on one occasion she visited a lawyer but couldn't initiate legal proceedings.

With so little self-love, she allowed herself to suffer the indignities of her husband's insensitive behaviors and to bear the public shame his *adulterous* relationship brought to their home. I helped her gain some understanding of the dynamics of her marital commitment and to develop a measure of self-assertiveness. But she continued to perceive herself as less lovely than Bruce. If sometime in the future Bruce again chooses to be unfaithful she is likely, but perhaps with more resistance, to relinquish herself to a similar process of psychological and emotional abuse.

Bernie and Gina

Let me now turn to a third case in which the absence of self-love resulted in a broken relationship. The relationship between Bernie and Gina presents a different look from the two just discussed. When Gina was referred to me she had been divorced from her first husband and was remarried. Both of her husbands had achieved the highest level of education required by their respective professions and were accorded appropriate public esteem. Gina worked in a career that required less education and gave her less social recognition. She was an attractive woman and won the love of these two men with her warmth, charm, and grace. During their courtships with Gina both men found her to be pleasant and easy to please. She demonstrated understanding and accepted their faults and irritable behaviors.

Following the rites of the marriage ceremony, her temperament and behavior changed radically. Bernie related to me that she seemed to look for reasons to criticize him, citing ineffective parenting, excessive drinking, failure to help her with the housework, and lack of consideration for her grown children. He could do nothing right, nothing to please her. She had no difficulty picking out the flaws in his person and behavior, but seldom had anything positive to say about him.

After three years of her emasculating treatment Bernie terminated the relationship. In his words, "Enough is enough, I can take no more." This, of course, did not surprise me. Any personal adequacy he possessed when he got married had been diminished by her scathing verbal attacks and, at times, by explosive pounding on his chest with her fists. Ending the relationship was the only way he felt he could restore his personal dignity and emotional stability.

Gina's worth lay in her physical beauty. Inside, she harbored frightening feelings of personal weakness and inferiority. It's a common practice in our society for individuals to conceal their feelings of inner ugliness behind an outer show of physical attractiveness and personal charm. This is a winning combination for pursuing love - *hide the bad, expose the good.* But our authentic self cannot remain hidden. It strains to be expressed and, in time, breaks the chains of discipline that bridle it.

When Gina's self-restraints collapsed, her true character surfaced. Her feelings of weakness and inferiority took the form of dominance and control over her more publicly acclaimed husband. She was an example of the truism that "powerless people seek power." Gina attempted to become a more powerful person by controlling the life of her spouse who had earned and legitimately exercised a fixed amount of power in his professional life.

112

Come Into My Life

Through her twisted thinking she had arrived at a distorted understanding of love. Gina had concluded that powerful people are also lovely people. She tried to get the power she lacked by controlling the person of power whom she married.

People who love themselves are secure in the power of their person and have no need or desire to create powerlessness in others. Love does not act in this way. Love always raises up; it never tears down. Love looks for and promotes the virtues of others; it doesn't look for their imperfections and lift them up as major disorders of personality. Love is supportive of people; it is not a mirror that reflects their frailties and faults.

By accentuating the flaws in her husband's behaviors and by drawing attention to the blemishes in his character, Gina was sending the message, "See, I am much lovelier than you." She insisted that her actions were expressions of love because, as she believed, Bernie would be a much lovelier person if he would be the person she hoped for him to become. Yet, love never uses unlovely actions or words to achieve its goals.

In all three cases the wives became less rather than more lovely in relating to their husbands. Carol, the servant of her husband and children, was obedient and fulfilled her roles and duties efficiently without complaint. She placed her wishes second to those of her husband. She was, of course, free to express her opinions and desires, but was obliged to accept Rob's decisions. She made life richer for other family members. While contributing to the loveliness of her family, Carol allowed her own beauty to become tarnished by living in the shadows of her husband and children.

For Dee, unconditional loving allowed Bruce to have an affair without risking the end of their marriage. Her sufferance and forbearance showed the emotional pain caused by her husband's rejection. Dee could not hide the sadness that filled her heart nor the shattered hopes that embraced her thoughts. She presented herself to those around her as crestfallen, longing for someone to bring cheer into her life. She seldom smiled, and lines of unhappiness were drawn across her face. Dee could not view herself as lovely, nor did she expect others to perceive her as lovely. Working with Dee, I learned that the loss of beauty is the price of submitting to abuse.

Gina, who hid the ugliness of her character behind a facade of warmth and friendliness during her courtship, let it surface soon after the marriage vows had been exchanged. Her wrath flowed freely against Bernie. There was no end to her fault-finding. Her nagging and complaining were such a part of her relationship style that she seemed to have them rehearsed. Although she was convinced that Bernie could become more lovely only if he submitted to a personality re-creation under her "skillful tutoring," it was her comeliness that changed. She was not aware that her own loveliness withered as she diminished the loveliness of her husband.

Equally significant in these relationships is the husbands' lack of self-love. Rob derived feelings of personal worth by being married to a woman who gave him more caring and a higher status than she gave to herself. Acting as a submissive servant, she led him to believe that he was her superior. The unconscious message he repeated to himself was, "I am an important man and the devotion of my wife proves it." Consciously, his thoughts carried a more noble message. "I am a good person and the way I diligently labor to provide for my wife and children proves it." This latter message could refute anyone who might point out to him the selfishness he chose not to hear from his unconscious communication.

Come Into My Life

Bruce's deficiency in self-love was evidenced by his need for the love of his wife and mistress. Insensitive to the hurt he inflicted upon Dee, Bruce believed that she should set aside her feelings and understand his anguish. He, afterall, must decide between two loves, one he had shared for 20 years and the other for just a few months. The two women were expected to wait until he had made his selection. He could claim the person he desired, but Dee and his paramour had no such choice. Each woman pleaded for his love. But Bruce treated their pleas simply as testimonies of love, which he used to confirm his belief that he was a special person. The unconditioned love of his wife and girlfriend made possible his continuing delusion, namely, "How lovely I must be."

Bernie did not need a servant nor the love of more than one woman to make him feel personally attractive. Rather, he sought pretty and charming women with social elegance and refinement. Feeling that he did not have these qualities, he reasoned that he would be regarded with esteem if he could win and hold the love of a beautiful woman who did have them. He used his professional status to lure Gina into a relationship only to discover in time, and too late, that she was a woman who had never nurtured inner beauty.

I tried to help all these spouses develop greater *self*-trust, *self*-esteem, and *self*-love. In the disguise of love, they were living together in egocentric relationships. Each was using the other to blunt the painful acknowledgment of the real inner person that threatened to break the bonds of their conscious control. For Carol, Dee, and Bernie the bonds broke. When they did not receive love, they felt weak and alone. Their self-regard diminished, despair set in, and they held themselves in contempt for not being worthy of love. I could not help them heal their relationships until their needs and dependencies, which had attracted them initially to their mates, had been eliminated and replaced with self-love.

They found the search for self-love to be rewarding and emerged from therapy with a clearer understanding of their identities, which included a deeper sense of personal dignity and importance. Each became a more self-validating person.

Initially their partners were reluctant to develop a greater appreciation of themselves as people with inherent worth and loveliness. They were satisfied with their relationships because they were receiving the need fulfillment essential for their happiness. They believed, and tried to persuade me to believe, that their spouses had "the problems" and that they were in therapy only to assist them with the resolutions of those problems.

Two of the couples, Carol and Rob and Dee and Bruce, accepted my treatment plan and therapeutic approach and used the insights they gained to become more self-loving. By ascribing more love and worth to themselves, they relied less upon their spouses for the continuing flow of unconditioned love to sustain their images of beauty. Freed from immersion in selves, the husbands and wives of both couples could look upon, and more objectively contemplate, the beauty they beheld in each other.

Love is attracted to loveliness; need is drawn to need-satisfaction. When love is inspired to act, the person who inspired it is the focus of that action. When need makes its demand, however, the person in whom it arises is the center of its absorbing attention. If love is activated, its energy flow is directed outward to the object of its loving. But not so with need. When it is set in motion, the flow of energy is away from others and inward toward self. And so the four people in these two relationships began to relate to each other with more loving because their needs for confirming loveliness from one another decreased. It was replaced with more love of self, hence, allowing love for their spouses to grow.

They discovered the underlying principle of love-bonded relationships. You cannot love another person if your need for that person is so pressing that it conceals the beauty to which love is attracted. You cannot love someone for whom you have a pressing need because that person then becomes only a means to an end. That end is you - the "lover" obsessed only with the needs of self.

I was unable to help Bernie and Gina save their relationship. Gina chose not to remain in therapy long enough to recover from the massive deficit in self-love which she had experienced for most of her life. And, as we would expect, her need to control and exert power over Bernie intensified when his need for her loving confirmation was gradually replaced by his self-affirming love.

He began to recognize his pattern of relating with women and no longer required a pretty woman to complete his maleness. Released from his neediness for a lovelier person to affirm him, he was able to look more deeply into the total person of this woman he had married. It did not take long for him to learn that Gina had few of the traits and qualities of a lovely person. He was embarrassed to have been deceived by her charming behavior and physical beauty. I could read in his face the statement his pride did not allow him to speak, "What a fool I have been!" Her need for Bernie remained as pressing as ever, but now he refused to be used for her selfish ends. The relationship, therefore, could not survive.

When thirst is quenched, we turn away the offer of water. Thirst represented Bernie's longing for feelings of worth. Because he could now satisfy this longing more from his newly developing self-love, he turned away from beautiful women whose love he had used to quench his emotional and psychological thirst.

Herein lies the risk of treating marital conflicts with deeper disturbances related to the self-concepts of the marriage partners. The mutual satisfaction of psychological needs is disrupted when the self-concept of only one spouse, in this case Bernie, is enhanced. His wife, in her continuing personal and psychological needy state, persisted in demanding behavioral changes that enabled her to maintain the "power" position in the relationship. The personal and emotional distance between them widened until eventually separation and divorce ended the agony of their stormy relationship.

When successful, however, treating these deeper disturbances results not only in reconciliation but also in a stronger bond within a loving relationship. And anything less is an unfair exchange for couples that invest their time, energies, and money in therapy.

* * *

"Physician heal thyself" is a proverb with sound wisdom. A healthy physician is a more effective healer of others. So, likewise "husband, wife, love thyself." You will then know love, trust love, and give the sincere love that your beloved will eagerly receive.

How do you give love to yourself? Not by looking into a mirror and saying to the person you see, "I love you." Not by

118

talking back to the self-censuring voice that keeps you feeling unworthy and unlovely. We love others by performing acts of love that increase their happiness and add to their well-being. In like manner, we show love for ourselves by doing those things that give us greater joy in living and make us physically, mentally, and spiritually well.

What are the acts of self-love that you can point to that bring you joy and wellness? By completing the exercise at the end of this chapter you will be able to answer this question. It will also give you a place from which to start your climb to a higher level of self-loving.

Exercise

CHART OF SELF-LOVE

Read each item carefully, consider the extent to which it is true for you, and place a check in the space that most appropriately applies. You may add to this list any of the other ways by which you exhibit love for yourself. Rate them and include them in your final score.

Consider love for yourself to be equal to the level of truth you have given to each item. An average score can be computed by adding up the scores for each statement and dividing that sum by the total number of items.

The score on your CHART OF SELF-LOVE will raise your level of awareness of how little or how highly you regard yourself as good and lovely. The results demonstrate the subtlety of how we hurt ourselves even when consciously we profess to have high self-regard and self-esteem. You may find that you will have to change your behaviors to bring about a greater agreement between *what you do for yourself* and *what you say about yourself.*

When you have read and completed the suggested task at the end of chapter ten, compare this score from your CHART OF SELF-LOVE with the results of the LOVE AT WORK ASSESSMENT QUESTIONNAIRE. I will be surprised if there is not a high correlation between the two, that is, the higher your score on self-love the greater will be the number of things you do to help your beloved "be" more of who she/he wants to become.

Acts of Self-Love	**33% True**	**66% True**	**100% True**
1. I give my body the rest it needs.	___	___	___
2. I keep my body and mind free from the harmful effects of alcohol.	___	___	___
3. I give myself the good feelings of coming to the aid of others in need.	___	___	___
4. I enrich my personal life by being friendly and by developing friendships.	___	___	___
5. I protect myself physically by fastening my safety belt and using safe driving habits.	___	___	___
6. I give my body mostly nutritious foods.	___	___	___
7. I keep my body and mind free from the harmful effects of drugs.	___	___	___
8. I keep my body free from the harmful effects of tobacco.	___	___	___
9. I relate to others by acting and speaking in ways that invite positive responses rather than hostile retaliations.	___	___	___
10. I give my mind rest by rescuing it from life's demands upon it - giving it allotted time for solitude.	___	___	___
11. I keep my conscience free from guilt by being true to my morals and values.	___	___	___
12. I place on my body only the work demands that it can reasonably tolerate.	___	___	___
13. I lighten my life by resolving conflicts and making decisions quickly rather than carrying them with me as a burden.	___	___	___
14. I give my mind the challenge and rigor			

Come Into My Life

Acts of Self-Love	33% True	66% True	100% True
of new learning.	___	___	___
15. I give respect to myself by not allowing others to physically, verbally, or mentally abuse me.	___	___	___
16. I minimize the effects of tension and stress of daily living on my mind and body by seeking a higher meaning for living.	___	___	___
17. I provide regular nurture for my spiritual life.	___	___	___
18. I give my body and mind the health benefits of regular exercise.	___	___	___
19. I give myself the self-respect and self-admiration that comes from setting goals and achieving them.	___	___	___
20. I admire myself as a parent because I give love to my children through my presence in their lives.	___	___	___
21. I do and say only those things that add to the beauty of my spouse.	___	___	___
22. I give myself the good feelings of accomplishment that come from completing what I start.	___	___	___
23. I give myself the good feelings that come from helping others to feel good about themselves.	___	___	___
24.	___	___	___
25.	___	___	___

Chapter Seven

Love's Victory

winning in love is a lifelong contest

Love is an ardent pursuer. The person in whose bosom it swells places the self second to the one from whom love is sought and to whom it is offered. A man and woman develop a deeply affectionate relationship only through a long and devoted courtship. While courting, they win each other's love, using a single strategy - displaying thoughtful and loving attention.

In their quest for love, they show only the favorable features of their personalities. They conceal much of themselves behind an exterior of the person they feel their beloved expects them to be. Their imploring behaviors are marked by personal sacrifices they consider necessary to assure love's victory.

Probably in no other life quest do we invest so passionately as we do in courting. It's goal has no parallel in human strivings. We fully understand that the beloved cannot be bought, earned, or forcefully taken. A man or woman must *win* the love of the beloved, who chooses to be won or not to be won. This choice is determined largely by the amount of trust that they place in the other's loving. Courtship, therefore, needs to be sufficiently long to allow for this trust to develop.

Even with a long period of courtship it is not always easy to accurately assess the sincerity of another's love. As I have mentioned, lovers are likely to conceal their unlovely qualities. They do this because they doubt the loveliness of their authentic selves. So in their pursuit of love they create *pseudo selves* that are more winsome and captivating. They do this even though true love is neither cunning nor deceptive.

This brings us to the problem that some men - more so than women - have with what I refer to as the "elusive lover." One man, in total frustration, described it to me this way. "Just when I felt I had successfully won her love, she escaped by retracting much of the love and commitment that she had given." This occurs because the woman does not yet trust the loving gestures of the man who is trying to win her love. Fearing rejection in the future, she removes the risk of an emotional hurt by keeping his pursuit in process. In this way she continually tests his love. The testing doesn't end until she is convinced that his love is genuine.

Kay – An Elusive Lover

My work with Kay, who was referred to me by her suitor, illustrates well the dynamics of this behavior. He was a respectable professional man who had been trying to win Kay's love for nearly a year. Yet, with all of his promises, gifts, and loving attention he was unable to convince her that his love was sincere.

Their relationship was harmonious and equally pleasurable for a couple of weeks and then, without announcement or provocation, Kay's behaviors changed. She broke social en-

124

gagements on short notice with flimsy excuses. She resisted his attempts to be affectionate and became uncommunicative. And most upsetting to him, she showed little concern about the confusion and emotional turmoil that she caused for him. Following several days of these behaviors, for no apparent reason, Kay renewed the warm relationship, almost as though nothing different had occurred. Her lover stated, "I feel like a bait on a fishing hook; she casts me out, draws me back in, and casts me back out again."

Kay admitted that she knowingly behaved this way. She did not intend to give him the security of her love until she was absolutely certain he intended to marry her. She began to trust his affections only after he had given her an engagement ring and they had set their wedding date. His willingness to commit himself to marriage enabled her to give herself to him in a consistently loving way.

We cannot harshly judge, nor should we be quick to censure Kay for the lack of trust she knowingly and intentionally demonstrated. She was protecting herself from a practice that is all too common in our society. In the ordinary course of most of life's challenges, our pattern is to win, briefly relish the victory, and then allow our prize to lose its value.

I cite here three examples of how carelessly we handle the trophies that we receive for our hard-fought victories. Rebellions are staged and wars fought to gain freedom. Freedom is the reward that downtrodden resistant fighters receive for their sacrifice. Yet, with the passing of time, they forget the value of the freedom they have won. Feeling secure with their possession, they lose their vigilance. Then, one day they awake to find that it has again been taken from them.

Athletes condition their bodies, discipline their minds, and aggressively compete against their opponents. They win the game and proudly accept a trophy for their victory. They hold it high over their heads for a few moments and then place it in a glass encasement for safe keeping. In time its surface becomes tarnished, and people walking by seldom take the time to stop and look at it.

Young people enroll in college, spend long hours completing assignments and attending classes. Four years later they excitedly walk across the stage, shake the hand of the college president and receive their diplomas. They, along with their friends and family, admire it briefly and then place it in a drawer or filing cabinet where it remains as a forgotten testimony of the hard work that earned it.

Time and again I have seen these same behaviors in men and women in their search for love. They win each other's love and then all too easily forget its value. And if a successful suitor takes his "victory prize" for granted, it is easy for another person to woo and steal his beloved. Likewise, when one or the other fails to be lovingly attentive, the loveliness that was attractive and charming becomes dull. The smiles on the lips, the sparkles in the eyes, the cheerfulness in the voice, and liveliness of the personality are gone. And, how easy it is to carelessly file the memories of the past joys of courtship in the hidden recesses of the mind rather than to relish the pleasures of a continuing love affair.

In all of these ways we tend to treat our beloved as we treat other conquests in life. We give more interest and time to the process of winning than we give in cherishing the prize of our victory.

The goal of love is not just to win the hand and heart of the beloved in marriage. It is to win the privilege and the honor of being the only lover that the beloved will have for the rest of his or her life. Marriage marks the end of the pursuit and also the beginning of a *lifelong* celebration.

With marriage comes new and different ways to shower love upon each other. Every opportunity to love is eagerly seized. Expressing love in acts of tenderness and thoughtfulness, in written and spoken words of adoration, and in sharing lives with joyous moods and lighthearted humor becomes the lifestyle of two lovers. They think about and appreciate the loveliness of each other and rejoice secretly and openly in their good fortune. And, in their elation they sense that their love can be even deeper. Rather than planning ways to siphon love from the other, each is always asking the self, "How can I love my loved one more?"

Although they win each other's love, neither views the victory as an entitlement, that is, claiming the other as a possession. A possession has no voice or choice in the way it is used by its owner. So, in love and marriage husband and wife are free to be who they need and desire to be. They are distinct persons, with different interests, values, opinions, personal aspiration, and daily lifestyles. Love readily acknowledges and accepts these differences.

When differences cause conflicts that obstruct one or both in their pursuit of "being," they are resolved with love. While searching for a resolution they don't behave in ways that erode each other's beauty. They don't use personal differences to justify reacting in an unlovely or uncomplimentary way. Rather, they use them to show how love continues to minister its affections even when it is powerless to control, shape, or influence the beloved.

If each loves the other, resolutions to conflicts are reached that may not always add to the loveliness of either spouse. But neither do they detract from the loveliness that is already there. When they ultimately resolve their disagreement they will have retained their beauty with the same luminous clarity that was present before the conflict surfaced.

Often when conflict occurs, I find that one spouse will say at some point, "You don't love me anymore." Censure that attacks the love commitment augments rather than resolves conflicts. Love that toils so hard to win doesn't relinquish its prize because of a disagreement.

Differences account for the special loveliness in people. The beauty of lovely people is their uniqueness. To win the love of another is, therefore, to possess a love that no one else shares. It is a one-of-a-kind love.

Looking again at our three illustrations, the struggle of free people to maintain freedom seemingly never ends. Athletes must win many events in order to have a victorious season. Students often are not content with their educational achievements until they have successfully earned several degrees. Individuals in all of these fatiguing labors are in a continuing process of winning. It is no different in our love relationships. Although married, we are in a life-long courtship.

When a couple stops courting, it is tempting for one or the other to embark on another search for love. This is the key that helps us to understand Kay's elusiveness. She would not allow herself to fall into the grasp of her lover until she was convinced that he would not pursue any other love.

Kay wanted to be certain that she would have no other rival after she had committed herself to him. Winning her hand in marriage was a one time victory, but winning her heart in love is a lifetime quest.

Come Into My Life

Because it requires so much attention and devoted care, there is only enough room in a person's life for one love. Unattended, love withers as the fruit of the vine without recurring sunshine and rain.

When I receive love from another, I am more than just "a face in the crowd." I sense the being of my lover as part of myself. This is what happens to two people in love. That animated life principle, with all of its thoughts, hopes, and wills, which each brings into the relationship, is so completely exposed that it can be known and shared by the other. So now I perceive the sensation of my spouse's spiritual being as having its origin within me, rather than having been imparted from her to me. Instead of being merely an admired trophy, this loving spirit that I have taken into my life becomes spiritually experienced as self.

It is this embodiment of another's spirit, whom we love, that makes their death so grievous. Some of the vital essence of our life is taken from us with the passing of a loved one. There is not as much liveliness, enthusiasm, and cheerfulness as there was when the beloved was present to arouse these qualities of the zestful life within us.

Two people in love define themselves, at least in part, in terms of the spirit of the other. Therefore, if the life of the one is in any way diminished, there is a corresponding loss of life within the other. This is love's victory, the two sharing a life of *becoming one.*

Has the passion of your relationship given way to the routine of a dull marriage? If so, it is because you have stopped laboring to win your beloved. When you have completed the following exercise, *To Win And Cherish*, you will know more clearly in which direction your relationship is moving.

Exercise

TO WIN AND CHERISH

For each of the nine statements below first read the description of the *reason* for getting married. Then, put the number from the rating scale (which most appropriately reflects how important it was for you) in the space at the beginning of each statement. Secondly, using the same process, indicate the *extent* to which your expectation has been fulfilled in your marriage. Then, follow the directions at the end of the exercise to learn if you and your spouse are still working to win the love of one another.

Reason For Marriage - (RFM)   **Extent of Fulfillment - (EOF)**

1 - Not Important   1 - Not Fulfilled
2 - Somewhat Important   2 - Somewhat Fulfilled
3 - Important   3 - Fulfilled
4 - Very Important   4 - Very Fulfilled
5 - Most Important   5 - Most Fulfilled

I chose to get married because:

1. Cultural Conformity – Society expects people to marry. When you reach a certain age and are not married, others tend to think that you have "something wrong with you." It's the socially and morally acceptable arrangement for having children. I want to be in the norm group.

        _____ RFM   _____ EOF

2. Commiseration/Compassion - I knew there would be times when I would be caught up in the "blues." It is comforting to have someone with whom to share my feelings. I need the compassion of a loved one when the way becomes hard. True compassion comes only from someone who loves you. Only the consolation of genuine love is able to heal.

        _____ RFM   _____ EOF

Come Into My Life

3. Covenant – It is important for me to be special in the life of another and to have one person who is special in my life. The "I"/"Thou" relationship is one that can be achieved only with reciprocal commitments of two people who love honor, and cherish each other.

_____ RFM   _____ EOF

4. Consolidation Of Assets – Two can live more cheaply than one. Two people who pool their money can afford more of life's necessities, as well as enjoy more of life's "extras." If one person becomes unemployed the other is able to provide for the flow of the family income.

_____ RFM   _____ EOF

5. Constancy – It is comforting to me to be able to trust the steadfastness of another's love. I experience greater personal stability when I invest myself in a relationship that provides a fixed and firm meaning to life that is larger than myself.

_____ RFM   _____ EOF

6. Convenience – Marriage allows for a division of responsibilities in the home. Skills I lack, my spouse may possess. When I am unable to perform my roles, my spouse is available to temporarily assume them.

_____ RFM   _____ EOF

7. Companionship – It is nice to know I always have a companion with whom to share activities and interests. A companion is the best antidote for loneliness. It's easier to walk the "rough road" with an understanding companion.

_____ RFM   _____ EOF

8. Conversation/Communication – It's lonely to have no one with whom to talk. My life's pleasant experiences are more enjoyable for me when I share them with one who rejoices with me. The thinking of two people provides a more complete understanding of an issue than does the thinking of one person.

   _____ RFM   _____ EOF

9. Procreation – My children will be raised in a loving environment. I want to have my lineage continued. I look forward to the joys and rewards of parenting. Life is happiest with laughing children to brighten my days.

   _____ RFM   _____ EOF

Review your responses. If you find greater fulfillment in items 1, 4, 6, and 9 than you do for items 2, 3, 5, 7, and 8, your marriage is probably more stable than is your love relationship. Perhaps you and your spouse have given up on your efforts to win the love of one another. If so, you may decide that now is the time to renew your courtship and bring love back into your marriage.

CHAPTER EIGHT

Love Is A Gift

love does not make receiving love a condition for giving love

The most quoted scripture of the Bible, the "love chapter," includes the phrase "...love seeketh not its own."[1] Love does not woo or indulge itself. When love gives itself to another, it doesn't insist on love in return. We can't force anyone to love us. Nor can we extract love from others by using love to get love. Love is given freely, with no strings attached. Love is a gift, not a medium of exchange. It comes from one person who chooses to give it to another who, in turn, decides to receive or not to receive it.

Mary

One of my patients nearly surrendered the choice to accept or refuse love because she didn't want to disappoint her insistent suitor. Mary was a widow for over 17 years. Her children were grown and lived hundreds of miles away. In her mid-fifties she met a gentlemen of the same age. John was a wealthy widower of five years. From the moment he met Mary, he determined that one day she would become his wife. So, in his most dashing manner, he began a whirlwind romance. The flurry of the courtship was breathtaking for Mary. And when he placed a beautiful and expensive diamond ring on her finger she did not resist. All this happened before Mary was able to clear away the fog of the romantic dream he created, and which blurred the realities of their relationship.

Over time, these realities came more sharply into focus. First of all, she would have to leave her teaching job, sell her home, move several states away, and develop a new circle of friends. She would be expected to adopt a different style of living, abandon her career and replace it with another purpose and meaning. Mary had always lived her life in a productive and unselfish way. So she could not become just a full-time consumer of the fruits of someone else's labors. Further, she found her deeply rooted religious beliefs in conflict with John's nominal confession of faith and intellectual concept of deity. These major issues, along with many minor ones, created a doubt that could not be silenced.

For several sessions Mary agonized over the decision to accept or reject John's gift of love. She was both humbled and grateful for his offering. Her dilemma was real. On the one hand, she could not receive his love without surrendering other loves. On the other hand, since she was a warm and caring person, she was reluctant to return the ring. She knew that giving it back would burst his dream. As she said, "I know it will break his heart." Not until she had returned the ring, however, was the weight of indecision lifted.

As so often happens, when one burden is lifted it is replaced with another. In this instance the burden of indecision, which she shed, was replaced with the weightiness of guilt. John accepted his rejection with the words, "I guess you couldn't love me enough." By stating his hurt in this way, he placed the blame on her for the failure of their love relationship to fully develop. But it was he who, in his haste to give love, did not allow her enough time to decide if she wanted to accept it. He had assumed that love repeatedly given should be received with love returned. The result of this assumption for both John and Mary was an embarrassing ending of their relationship.

An honest response to his offerings of love could have been given in this way, "Your love for me is greater than my love for you, but I do care very much for you. I would like to love you as you love me, but at this time I can't lead you to believe that I truly do."

Her failure to express her feelings led to a grievous misunderstanding. John believed that she loved him with the same love that he gave to her. And in the beginning of the relationship she did give him love even as she received it. But in time, as she became lost in the maze of her feelings, she found that she wanted less and less to be together with him. She withheld her verbal and behavioral displays of affection which earlier she had given. Her interest in sharing in joint plans and activities turned into apathy. John was left with pieces to a puzzle that he could not put together. All because Mary, caught up early in a romantic reverie, had surrendered her choice to say "no" to his love.

I recall a 25-year-old male patient who was able to capture this insight into the nature of loving. He summarized one of our discussions with the simple statement, "You can't force the destiny of a relationship." Succinctly and accurately, he stated why he could not develop a relationship with a woman whom he deeply loved. He found himself in love with a person who could not return his love with the same quantity that he gave to her.

He reacted to her reluctance by loving and pursuing more fervently. Like putting more fuel on a fire to get a greater flame, he gave more and deeper affection expecting to arouse and evoke greater love from her. But it didn't work that way. Predictably, the emotional distance between them grew wider. He was losing a young lady whom he impassionedly wanted to win.

With this new understanding of love, he gradually retreated. Changing his approach gave her the opportunity she needed to assess his loveliness and to test her own love for him. Because she no longer needed to defend against his relentless advances toward her, she was free to move toward him as her love impelled her to do. During the months that followed, their love relationship developed.

This young suitor could have avoided his initial disappointment. He mistakenly assumed that because his love was so pure and deep he could shape the relationship for both of them. He learned that the sincerity of his love could not replace her freedom to choose - to receive or not to receive his love.

I had no doubt that he was deeply in love. He had worked hard to express his love for this woman who had taken hold of his passion and won his commitment. However, "to labor in love" doesn't mean burdening one's self in servitude in order to "earn" love that must be given freely. We give love only because the loveliness in the other leads us to do so.

It's not always easy to determine if another individual's love for us is genuine. I have worked with many innocent victims of love's intent who can testify to its misleading character in the lives of self-absorbed predators. They were enticed into believing that the loving expressions of their suitors were the actions of loving people. In time, they discovered how acts of love can be used by self-serving people to achieve selfish ends.

Come Into My Life

Innocent people, needing to be loved, readily return love and commit to a relationship when seduced by the lovely behaviors of another person. It is not until their loved one begins withholding those loving actions and replacing them with indifference that deception becomes apparent. Then it is too late for these unsuspecting victims to avoid the emotional hurt that lay at the end of their "lovers" betrayal.

Self-seeking is easily concealed within the cloak of loving words and gestures. Individuals whose need for love is pressing are the most vulnerable to the duplicity and manipulation of selfish love.

How do we know when love is a gift from a lovely person? This is not always easy to determine. In the chapter, *Love At Work*, the reader will find many helpful hints for making this determination.

Love and deceit do not come from the same source. Anyone who tries to ascertain the loveliness of another person must observe carefully the consistency of that person's behaviors, paying particular attention to the types and frequencies of the breakdowns between love professed and love expressed.

The love-bond is only as strong as the authenticity of the love of the two persons who have created it. And authentic love is the product only of lovely people. As I have stated, we cannot demand, we cannot force the return of love for the love that we give to another. We can only create and maintain a personal loveliness in which the love we declare and the love we display are the same. This type of loveliness is beautiful and magnetic. When we enter the sphere of its influence we cannot resist its lure. A love relationship that grows out of such a compelling attraction will not succumb to the legion of forces that lie in wait, always ready to enter in where harmony reigns and replace it with discord and division.

A love-bond is strong only when two persons contribute equally to the binding process. Each then moves towards the other at the same pace. At a point that cannot be pre-established, they mutually declare their love. All along the path to this goal, with each other's help, they appraise the love received and the love given.

They will know when the love-bond has been developed because the statements, "*I* am in love," and "*we* are in love," will have the same meaning. Each can speak for both, as well as for self, with certainty because they have contributed equally to the formation of their bond. And they have done so with the full awareness of one another's gifts of love. Each is able to say confidently, "he loves me," or "she loves me." They have no need to speculate about the other's love. Likewise, they don't carry the needless burden of continually proving their love, simply to remove lingering doubts in one another.

"Game playing" is not part of a love-bonded relationship. Because the goal they seek is so intensely cherished, neither person would jeopardize it with deception and dishonesty. For even if they were to establish it, using deceptive loving, their love-bond could not be sustained because it would be built on a weak foundation - distrust.

Since our feelings are keenly responsive to the words and behaviors of those who profess to love us, much emotional hurt is inflicted when we are willfully deceived. Love does not play with feelings, using them as toys. Our feelings are too easily injured to be kicked around as a child might treat its teddy bear. Every effort is made, therefore, to handle one another's feelings with respectful consideration. So, we *never use unlovely behaviors* to win love.

Come Into My Life

Exercise

MY LOVE I GIVE TO YOU

Listed below are nine different ways to give love to your spouse. Item number ten invites you to use any additional ways which you may choose to present your beloved with a gift of love. In the days and weeks ahead select one of these *love gifts* and give it to your beloved. Continue your giving until you have completed the entire list. After each presentation answer the following questions.

1. Did I expect to be appreciated?
2. Did I feel, "now it's your turn?"
3. Reflect on your feelings after giving each gift - did I feel elated, more self-loving, drawn closer to my beloved, etc.?
4. Did it make me more excited about giving more gifts of love?

MY GIFTS OF LOVE

1. The gift of a pleasant mood and a cheerful disposition.
2. The gift of a warm hug and tender kiss when not expected.
3. The gift of sharing in an activity that pleases your beloved even if it is not so important to you.
4. The gift of arranging a break for you and your beloved from a busy and tedious routine.
5. The purchase of a gift that is given not to celebrate a birthday, Christmas, or an anniversary.
6. The gift of a "surprise outing" that you know your beloved will enjoy.
7. Write your own little poem of love and give it with your words of love.
8. Give your beloved his or her most favorite expression of sexual love.
9. Give yourself to your beloved for a full day to do as he or she plans.
10. Give love in any other way that you feel is special.

139

CHAPTER NINE

Love Me And Let Me Be

love delights in the stimulation of differences

When I ask husbands and wives how they know they are in love, generally I hear the same answers, although stated in different ways. One person, who usually speaks for both, says, "Oh we have the same interests and like the same type of music. We enjoy doing the same things and being active. We both like our privacy. We are not the socializing and partying type. We are just so much alike."

Is *likeness* the bond which binds love between a man and a woman? Suppose one member of a couple develops an interest or engages in an activity that the other does not particularly like, or begins to enjoy the company of others to escape the boredom of seclusion. Will their love be deep enough to accommodate these dissimilarities?

Love accepts the "oneness" of the relationship, but also acknowledges that each person in the relationship is clearly distinguishable. A husband and wife may be emotionally and personally enmeshed in their love, but each must acknowledge the other as different.

I have noticed many times that when one spouse decides to make personal changes in his or her lifestyle, changes that do not affect the life of the other spouse, that spouse, nevertheless, objects to the changes. The objection is usually expressed by withholding love. The message within the objection is clear, "If you want me to love you, you must *be like me.*"

When I confront this resistance by a wife or a husband to the other's changing behaviors, I ask, "Isn't this really love of self, reflected from the life of the other who is the mirror image of yourself?" From here we move to the theme, *Love Me And Let Me Be.*

In a love relationship each person is unique. Being different doesn't mean drifting away from a loving partner. Differentiation signals a need to grow, develop, or unfold according to the individual's potential and choice of direction.

Ann and Bob

In therapy, Ann sought to become more of the person she felt was still hidden inside. Bob, her husband, was a successful businessman. While he was climbing the ladder to career success, she fulfilled the roles that supported his individuation. Ann was the hostess who planned the parties to entertain his business associates and clients. She accepted his expectations for her - to be a wife, a homemaker, and the mother of their children. She said she enjoyed being the primary parent, rearing their two sons and a daughter. Likewise, homemaking was a pleasant responsibility. Still, Ann felt that there was more of her yet *to become.*

Ann didn't have the time in her busy schedule to develop marketable skills necessary for a professional career. So she worked as a jewelry clerk in a large and fashionable department store. This was the first assertive step in her plans to be her own person.

Bob, in time, accepted her need *to become* and began to involve himself in her "becoming process." He did some of the grocery shopping and occasionally prepared meals. By encouraging his wife to walk outside of his shadow, he was helping her to discover a part of herself she had never known. Bob had accepted the message of love that Ann learned from therapy and had shared with him - "Don't walk behind me and don't walk in front of me. Walk only beside me."

*   *   *

It's not easy to distinguish a person who stands in a shadow. Several years ago, in a public meeting, I innocently made the mistake of placing one person in the shadow of the other. In a departmental meeting, I introduced a married couple, both of whom had joined the professional staff at our university. I presented first the husband, giving his personal background and the position for which he was hired. Then I introduced his spouse saying, "this is the wife of our new director of..." Before acquainting the department members with some of her personal and professional history, and of her new role at the university, I asked them to know her first as a partner in a marriage relationship.

Following the meeting, she tersely reminded me that she expected to be known as the individual *she is* and not as the "wife" of another professional. Her husband had lovingly encouraged her to develop her own identity. Without intending to do so, I had detracted from the clarity of that identity.

Love doesn't allow one spouse to use wealth, influence, position, or fame to create an identity for the other spouse. The spouse with status may choose to be identified with it. The other, however, must be free to create a self that is distinguishable, one that is his or her own. That self may not be as prestigious or as socially enviable, but it has been self-chosen.

In many instances, a man and a woman with different levels of educational achievement marry and have a happy loving relationship. I worked with such a couple prior to their marriage to help them form a stronger love-bond. The man had 22 years of academic education in a highly specialized profession. His fiancee had 12 years plus an additional year of vocational training. Their educational/professional difference was not a significant treatment component. Her career was just as self-fulfilling as was his. The prestige attributed to his position became unimportant in his therapeutic encounter with love.

Society plays a much greater role in "match-making," than we might suspect, by elevating certain professions to a higher status than others. It is not unusual, then, for individuals to fall in love first with the status and secondly with the person who has earned it. They hope to combine love, money, honor, and even power in the same relationship. But, like oil and water, these don't mix. They discover that the love in the relationship is little more than an illusion. Their love for each other becomes lost and cannot compete with these other loves.

People attain socially designated status symbols because they have placed them first in their order of priorities. They are their first love. When they marry, their spouses become the second love. Not satisfied with second place and feeling slighted,

144

their spouses strive to become first. The resistance they encounter contains an unmistakable message, *Love Me And Let Me Be.*

Jim and Susan

The case of Jim and Susan gives us good insight into the clash that occurs when one person tries to alter the "being" of another. From the time Jim was a teenager he worked hard to learn the building construction business, primarily from on-the-job experience. His goal was to advance as far as his experiential knowledge would take him. In time he became a construction supervisor, responsible for the beginning and completion of total building projects.

After 15 years of being a "second love" Susan entered therapy to deal with her anger and frustration. She described Jim as "insensitive" and "non-caring." Jim resisted her efforts to change him by quietly going about his business, holding fast to his resolve to advance his career. He was rewarded with a prestigious position, supervising building projects in a territory covering several states. Unable to draw him away from his first love, Susan considered divorce. But with therapy, for nearly a year, I helped them avoid divorce by understanding the dynamics that were destroying their relationship. Jim began to show more love to Susan, and without sacrificing his career ambitions. Satisfied with his more generous offerings of love, Susan no longer felt compelled to change the "person" he is and always will be.

Conflicts always occur when one spouse criticizes the other's behaviors, values, or style of relating. With some couples, conflicts take on a passive character. In order to preserve

145

harmony, the spouse under attack chooses not to respond angrily. He or she knows that such a response will simply fuel the disagreement, and so reacts with a smile or nod of the head. The resistance to change is manifested by silence. This was how Jim coped with Susan's insistence that he alter his life according to her guidelines. His choices were limited. Either he could change and become someone he was not, or remain true to himself and resist - actively or passively. Active resistance would have widened their emotional distance. His passive noncompliance did not draw them closer, but it did keep their disagreements from erupting into unmanageable outbursts of tempers.

But the tension continued to seethe within each spouse. Hostile encounters were prevented, but not without the cost of inner stress that always accompanies this type of anxiety management. Unyieldingly, Jim was saying, "I will be me. *My being* is not open to discussion and compromise."

Like many couples, Susan, citing Jim's silence, had reduced the problem to one of poor communication. In such situations, however, the messages are quite clear. Jim accurately understood what she was saying to him, "I don't like you the way you are, and you ought to change." She in turn had received a message which she understood but chose to ignore. It was simple and clear, "I am going to be me; love me as I am."

In most instances, spouses in conflict hear what each other is saying. They just choose not to hear the messages. Jim wanted to hear his wife say, "I love you the way you are." Susan wanted to hear an affirmation of love from Jim that said, "Because I love you, I will become what you desire."

One of the major roles of a therapist is to clarify messages. I have never been able to help a husband and wife move towards reconciliation until each has learned to truly know the other.

146

Come Into My Life

The message which each communicates and the other chooses not to hear rings loudly and clearly session after session: "This is who I am."

* * *

The story of Cinderella never loses its appeal. One of the popular themes in literature and in drama is the love relationship that develops between persons of unequal status in society. The response of a reader in a Dear Abby column describes clearly how love is elevated to a position above social standing.

> "Dear Abby: I read with amusement the letter from *On the Fence in Waukegan, Ill.*, the professional career woman who is dating a man who has only a high school education and works in a warehouse.
> She said, 'He treats me like a queen, but I'm concerned that perhaps he is too simple for me and I might get bored.'
> Well, I have some advice for her: If he's as good to you as you say he is, and you love him - marry him.
> I am a college professor who can lecture fluently in five languages, and I've been happily married for 10 years to a truck driver with an eighth-grade education.
> Intelligence has nothing to do with the level of schooling; decency and caring have nothing to do with the kind of work a man does; and loyalty has nothing to do with the size of a paycheck.
> Perhaps the old saying, 'opposites attract,' is true. My husband has brought more joy into my life than I ever had when I was previously married to another educator."
>
> -Opposite But Equal in Ohio[1]
> (taken from the DEAR ABBY column by Abigail Van Buren.
Distributed by UNIVERSAL PRESS SYNDICATE. All rights reserved)

147

This woman states that one person is not "looking up," nor is the other "looking down." They are persons of equal worth "looking out" at each other with a love that embraces the goodness and beauty that drew them together. These two lovers resisted society's pressure to find love within "your own class." The lines between their social strata were erased by a genuine love for each other. And being equals as individuals, they are *one* in love because they allowed each other "to be."

Ray and Jane

I always find it personally gratifying when a patient captures insights and converts them into attitudinal and behavioral changes. I experienced this with Jane, following a year of very regular and intense therapy. She came into my care longing for a closer, warmer relationship with her husband whom she loved. Ray, like Jane, was a professional person who loved his wife and children. However, unlike Jane, who spent most of her non-work hours parenting the children and in homemaking activities, Ray used his free hours in a hobby apart from other family members. With the exception of his emotional distancing from the family, Ray was a good husband and father, providing for the personal and physical comfort of Jane and the children. He participated willingly in therapy and made some changes that drew him more emotionally close to his family. Yet, it was not with the depth or consistency for which Jane had hoped.

Toward the end of our therapy, Jane summarized her thoughts and feelings about their relationship. It had not changed significantly, but now she looked upon it with new understanding and acceptance.

Come Into My Life

There he goes again -
  That beautiful butterfly yearning and
  searching for his freedom and solitude.
How we all cry inside for a chance to catch
  more than just a glimpse from afar.
He teases us as he touches our lives, then
  flies away again.
Run for the net and maybe we can make him stay -
  just for a little while.
Maybe he will show us his colors, share his
  thoughts, and include us in his dreams.
But would the capture be fair?
We can't make him stay -
  not only is it selfish, but it would
  stifle *his search* for meaning.
I guess *true love* is letting go -
  of the wants, the needs, and the desires,
  and allowing the butterfly *to be* -
  as much as it hurts.[2]

In her soliloquy, Jane conveys a passionate longing to share more of Ray's life and his inner thoughts and dreams. But she knows that her love means she cannot stifle his search for meaning nor deny his "being." Leaving therapy, Jane understood more clearly what together we set out to achieve - her love was only as genuine as her resolve to allow her beloved *to be.*

Exercise

MY PERSONAL GUIDE TO 'BEING'

Who do you want "to be?" When you have completed the following inventory, the person you want "to be" will be more clearly defined for you. This, then, becomes your *PERSONAL GUIDE TO BEING.* The inventory contains 10 of life's priorities. If there are any priorities that you feel are missing from the list, you may add them and include them in the ranking process.

Directions

Rank the following statements according to your personal preference. Number one is the most preferable, number two is the second most preferable, and so on. The definition for each statement of interest has been provided. Read each carefully before making your ranking.

When you and your spouse have completed your personal guides, share them with each other. Use the results as a discussion tool to teach one another why these preferences are important to you. Explain how you are, or are not, fulfilled in those areas of your "being" that are most, or very important, to you. Discuss how you can love each other without detracting from the "being" of your beloved while pursuing your own "being."

1. _____ *to be* open to my feelings and aware of my personal traits.
2. _____ *to be* alive in the expression of myself.
3. _____ *to be* in good physical health.
4. _____ *to be* a good parent.
5. _____ *to be* helpful in making my community a good place to live.
6. _____ *to be* religious in life, not just in the church.
7. _____ *to be* knowledgeable in a specific career.
8. _____ *to be* a friend of others and share in their lives.
9. _____ *to be* comfortable with the world's finer things.
10. _____ *to be* personally a part of the world shown on television and in books and travelogues.

Definitions

1. Developing emotionally and personally, being open to your full range of feelings, sharing them with another, accepting yourself as a whole person with strengths and weaknesses.
2. Engaging in hobbies and personal interest activities in which you use free time alone, with the family, or with other people.
3. Maintaining good health by combining proper diet, abstinence from harmful habits - smoking, alcohol/drug use, careless auto driving, and so on - and engaging in regular and rigorous exercise.

Come Into My Life

4. Having children and parenting in a home in which both parents assume responsibility for their care, growth, and development.
5. Involving yourself in the life of the community, working within civic organizations to achieve community improvement or to provide public services.
6. Practicing a religious faith, going beyond the form and ritual of a weekly worship service, translating your beliefs into practice.
7. Pursuing a higher education, perhaps earning a degree, or securing specialized vocational training to achieve both a better and more stable employment.
8. Joining with others and interacting formally and informally, sharing and enjoying the lives of others through an event or activity.
9. Achieving a comfortable life style with the pleasures of affluence and additional trimmings, such as expensive automobiles, larger house, brand name clothing, and so on, willing to work long hours to fulfill this desire.
10. Traveling and vacationing away from home as the preferable way to use time away from work, willing to set aside the needed money to enjoy this type of recess from your daily work routine.

CHAPTER TEN

Love At Work

love toils to create loveliness

Love has no being until it is put into action. Although this is a basic principle, many husbands and wives hold their love for each other within themselves as a pleasant, inactive feeling. They can't see one another's love because they don't show it in loving behaviors. They say, "I love you" and then fail to offer works of love to support their words of love.

Love doesn't exist in the passive mood. It doesn't wait to be set in motion by the loving of another. Containing its own source of energy, love moves toward the person whose loveliness arouses it to action.

Love is never hurtful, and so it always directs me to relate to my loved one with the question, "What will be the effect of my words and my behaviors in the life of my beloved?" Love is never inconsiderate. It doesn't try to excuse insensitive blunders with phrases such as, "I guess I wasn't thinking." Love doesn't try to justify an oversight with "good intentions" for the hurt caused by thoughtless behaviors or words. It doesn't act before thinking. Love doesn't try to excuse habitual, unkind behavior by continually requesting forgiveness. Love is reliable and consistent - the same today as it will be tomorrow. The one who receives love recognizes it immediately through the joy it creates. Love is real, not found in the hollow phrases of the poet, but in the personal devotion of one who gives self to enhance the beauty of another. It is always found laboring for the pleasure of its beloved who has laid claim upon it. Love contemplates the loveliness of the one who has kindled it, and then quickly goes into action.

Early in therapy, I ask the question, "Do you love your wife/husband?" It is important to establish that love is the foundation for a long-term relationship. Without mutual love, a relationship collapses under the demands that two individuals place upon it.

Answering this question, a husband said decisively, "Yes I do." Later in the session, during a lively exchange, he told his wife, "You're a very *specious* woman, but of course you don't know what that means!"

I interrupted their heated debate and reminded him, "You just told me that you love your wife, and now you've hurt her by saying she hides her true self, a self which you don't see as lovely."

I wanted him to be aware of the contradiction between his profession of love and his statement that was intended to inflict an emotional hurt. Confused and embarrassed, he rebutted feebly, "Well, I was just expressing the way I feel."

He was doing just that, expressing hateful feelings. By doing so, he detracted from the loveliness of his wife whom he said he loved. His words created an image of a person who would be less appealing to him. Without intention, he diluted his love for her. Being less lovely, she aroused less love in him for her. *This is not love at work.*

This young husband was confused by his wife's self-description and the person he saw in her behaviors and words. He had all the pieces, but he couldn't put them together to complete a picture that made sense. So he attacked his wife for causing his confusion. Rather than asking her to help him bring order to his mental disarray, he chose, instead, to punish her by accusing her of being a "specious" person. Although she seemed to be a good person, he became angry because he couldn't grasp her goodness.

Love, in this instance, would have entreated the beloved by saying, "Help me to understand." Love doesn't convert inner turmoil into anger and then heap that anger upon the person with whom one shares a love-bond.

Love guides its actions by the answer to the question, "What can I do to make my loved one's life fuller, richer, and more complete?" The work and goal of love is to enhance. In a love relationship each person tries to determine the other's need or desire to become more personally fulfilled and enriched. With this knowledge, love petitions, "Let me help you become."

Individuals in love are the servants of love. The loveliness of each commands and directs the love in the other to perform its work. This love readily accepts its commission because it is excited with its role in the life of the beloved. It labors not as a duty, but as a privilege. When activated, love is a tireless servant, fulfilling its many roles. The vision of its goal won't let it rest until it has done all that is possible to add to the being of the other. Only then does it take a respite from its work.

The case of Jim and Susan (discussed earlier in the Chapter *Love Me and Let Me Be*), a couple in therapy with me for more than a year, gives us some excellent insight in the nature of an avowed love that was "sleeping on the job." During twenty years of marriage with Jim, Susan had been a good mother to her son and, occasionally, was a foster parent. She was a faithful, unassuming homemaker.

155

Susan came to therapy feeling she was too physically and financially dependent on Jim. She decided to enroll in college to prepare herself for a teaching career in public education. Jim's response was, "It's OK as far as I'm concerned." Still, he suggested that she should find some work to pay for her education. Then he asked her, "Do you think you can handle both school and work?"

Susan perceived immediately his lack of support for her in this exciting new venture. Tearfully, she said to me, "At first I got sad and then I got mad." She sensed that secretly he hoped she would abandon her plans. So it was apparent that she would be alone if she attempted to pursue higher education to complete herself in a career.

Jim loved her, but not with the devotion that inspires the question, "What can I do to help my wife achieve her goal?" Without this question, his love was not summoned to action. So, without Jim's loving assistance, Susan set out alone to earn a college degree. In time, her husband provided some financial aid and encouragement. But we are left to ponder, was his commitment the work of love at its highest level of exertion?

*   *   *

Like the beauty of roses when their petals fully unfold, there is more loveliness in all persons who blossom to their fullest. There is more beauty to behold and a more complete person to be loved. The florist prepares the soil, plants the rosebush, prunes its boughs, provides moisture, and adds nutrition so that in time a completely mature rose will burst into bloom. It is admired and loved for itself. It has only its beauty and pleasant fragrance to give to the patient horticulturist who is responsible for its being.

In like manner, the lover does everything to enhance the beauty of the beloved. The beloved responds to the loving attention, saying, "I am grateful for all that you have helped me to become. In return for your labors I give you my loveliness. As I have received, even so do I give. My beauty is for you to behold, because without you I would not be who I am. I rejoice in my completeness, knowing that it is the fruit of your love."

Exercise

LOVE AT WORK
ASSESSMENT QUESTIONNAIRE

Using the result of YOUR PERSONAL GUIDE TO BEING, which you completed in the chapter, *Love Me and Let Me Be*, respond as directed for each of the following items.

1. Are you able to *feel*, not just *observe* or *know*, how important it is to your beloved to be fulfilled in the highest ranked priorities in his/her life? Can you get caught up in the passionate longing, with some of the same excitement, of your beloved's desire, and even need, to include the fulfillment of these interests in his/her *personal being*? Reflect on these two questions and arrive at an honest appraisal of your feelings.

2. How do you help your beloved to bring his/her "being" to fruition? Prepare a list of what you do and the attitudes you use to provide help to your husband/wife *to be* fulfilled in each of the higher ranked priorities.

3. Compare your list with the list your mate has prepared in which he/she has set down the ways by which he/she *would like for you to help.*

4. Discuss ways by which you can reduce the differences between the two lists.

5. Look at your own behaviors and list the things you do and the attitudes you show that make it difficult, if not impossible, for your beloved *to be*. That is, how is your lifestyle hindering your husband/wife from living the style he/she needs to live to reach a higher level of *personal being*?

6. Discuss ways by which each of you can make changes, putting your love to work without taking away from you own *beings*. Set them down on paper as a reminder of the mandate from love to act in love.

CHAPTER ELEVEN

Love Understands

*love is the patient confidant
that hears the silence of the heart*

Behind every marital conflict is the unspoken conviction that "he /she doesn't understand me." Whatever the words, this is the message I hear when I listen to spouses' exchange of complaints. Frustrated by their inability to elicit understanding, they stop listening to each other. Therapy then deteriorates into a "talkathon," with each filibustering to promote a position the other doesn't want to hear.

Everywhere, we find ourselves drowning in a flood of talk. We long to be understood. Instead, we are told to listen and to try to understand. We insist that others understand us, but we aren't willing to be understanding.

People enter into therapy because they know that their therapist will listen to them in a way that no other person does. Patients stay committed to the therapeutic process because the therapist has successfully conveyed the message, "I understand you." When we feel understood we return again and again to the source of that good feeling.

It's shameful that so many people in our society don't receive understanding unless they *buy it from a professional listener*. People are so engrossed in their own lives that they can't invest personally in the lives of others, regardless of how great the need. We shouldn't be surprised at the immense demand for therapy. The lonely and the alienated long for the understanding their therapist provides.

I know all too well the irritation of the wife who repeats the same monotonous refrain about her husband's faults. Or the impatience of a husband whose persisting complaint is his wife's nonstop nagging. They come for therapy because they know they will never get understanding from one another. Their repeated demands for the other to listen have fallen on deaf ears. I am aware that the role implicitly assigned to me is to be the channel through which the husband comes to understand the wife, and the wife is moved to understand the husband.

Because I care, and because the therapeutic process requires it, I try first to fully understand the husband and wife as individuals before attempting to help them heal their relationship. Listening to them elaborate in detail each other's faults, I discover how little understanding they actually have of one another. In a very few sessions I learn to know them in a way that neither has come to know the other. And, more than a collection of personal data, my knowledge is a deep and sensitive appreciation of how they are wrestling with their personal conflicts. I understand their needs, pains, fears, hopes, values, and disappointments. Without this understanding, I cannot help them to control the emotionally disruptive forces that are destroying their relationship.

Kathy and Ben

When Kathy, 30 years old and married for ten years, came to me, she was painfully coping with her husband's refusal to have children. Kathy, along with a sister and brother, was reared in a loving and warm family, and she had many good memories of shared times during the 20 years she lived in the home.

On the other hand, her husband, Ben, also 30, grew up in a home in which the primary nurturing parent, his mother, was cold, distant, and suffered from emotional and mental disorders. His father was a capable provider but had little time to spend with Ben and his older sister. Home, for Ben, was not a pleasant memory, and he never knew the beauty and innocence of childhood.

From the beginning, Ben made it clear he did not want to be a father. Kathy married him, believing in time she could change his mind. Ten years later he was as adamant, if not more so, in his feelings about children as on the day they were married. He viewed children as a liability in his quest for success in his aviation career. Kathy thought about her remaining child-bearing years. If she were to divorce and remarry, another three or more years could be lost, leaving only a few years in which to start a family. Her predicament was compounded by the continuing love she felt for Ben. He, too, said he loved Kathy but not in the same way he did earlier in their marriage.

In individual sessions I worked with each spouse as they shared their hurt and confusion. Only when they began to feel understood were they emotionally willing and ready to try to understand. In time they discovered the strength and inflexibility of one another's value system. They understood that they couldn't expect each other to give up values so deeply rooted without losing parts of themselves - a conflict rooted in *Love Me And Let Me Be.*

I asked each of them, "Aren't you so absorbed in your intense desire that you can't understand your beloved's equally intense desire?" Accepting this, they stopped trying to force each other to renounce the life-directing values which lay at the center of their conflict.

In time, they amicably divorced. Some months later Kathy was again dating, hoping to meet a man wanting a home and children. Ben, in the meantime, was dating a young woman who had received a degree in engineering and, like himself, was pursuing a career in aviation.

If you have been reading this account carefully, there is one truth that you have not missed: *We can't be understanding until we have first been understood*. When Ben and Kathy had been given the opportunity to be understood - in this instance by me, their therapist - they were then emotionally ready to understand each other.

I asked myself these questions: Why couldn't Ben and Kathy receive understanding from one another? Why were they choosing not to be touched by the longings and feelings they were trying to share with each other? Why didn't they convert their professions of love into actions of love? The only answer is that their love for each other was not strong enough to compete with the strength of the personal visions that were dominating their lives. In joint sessions we worked to temper the intensity of the desires that grew out of these visions and which monopolized their feelings and thinking. Then, under the moderating influence of a slowly developing but responsive empathy, they began to hear the emotional heartbeat of each other's deepest yearnings. As they attempted to understand one another, they received more understanding from the other.

*   *   *

Come Into My Life

Husbands and wives must have faith in the love-bond that brought them together in marriage and which will hold them together when they temporarily lose faith in one another. If they do not let love do its work, then mediators, commonly called marriage counselors, are invited to resolve the conflicts for them. The role tacitly assigned to these marriage "mediators" is to understand the viewpoints of both parties and to make objective judgments.

As a love relationship therapist, I can't allow myself to fill this role. I can't let myself be pressured to assume a responsibility which only they should fulfill. Rather, I take the appropriate role of helping them restore the strength of their love-bond. It has been weakened by their impassioned personal desires which hold them captive to unyielding self-indulgence.

Strengthening the love-bond requires the capacity to understand. Over the years I have conducted many marital enrichment seminars for couples who are, for the most part, in love and happily married. I have learned from these seminar experiences that the ingredient missing most from relationships, that are otherwise stable and secure, is patient understanding through focused listening. After years of marriage, husbands and wives develop the habit of listening without understanding. They no longer discern the message their ears mechanically hear.

To help them become better listeners, I structure my seminars to include a "listening and understanding" exercise. This activity sets the tone for the entire marital enrichment weekend. I ask each couple to find a secluded area, free from interruptions and bothersome noises. Each person has a role. First, one spouse is designated as the understanding listener; the other is seeking to be understood. If the wife is the first to talk, she selects a personal issue about which she feels deeply and takes as much time as needed to share it with her husband. He demonstrates that he hears and understands, both behaviorally (keeping eye contact, nods of the head, smiles) and verbally (clarifying, reflecting, uncritical questioning, and restating.) The listener is instructed not to react defensively, give advice, offer solutions, make judgments, or in any other way project the self into the issue that the spouse is presenting. Only when the wife is satisfied that she has been understood, are the roles reversed and the exercise repeated.

The discipline of listening for understanding, even in the structured situation described above, is not as easy as it appears to be. Typical comments from individuals who have participated in this listening activity include: "It's hard not to want to express your own ideas or opinions;" or, "I broke every rule you gave us for listening;" or, "I had a hard time controlling my impulse to interrupt and correct what she was saying."

It's difficult for people to listen and understand because they haven't learned to practice self-denial. In one sense a good listener has "non-being." In order to personally and emotionally understand another person, I must be able to merge with the "being" of that person. My thinking and feeling must be replaced by the discipline of thinking and feeling with the individual who is speaking to me.

Students in the helping professions learn to listen in this way because it is a critical skill they must master in order to achieve empathic closeness with their clients. But two individuals in love do not practice self-denial because it is a professional necessity. They practice it because lasting love requires it. Through understanding, they learn to know one another more completely, and their love more deeply permeates their lives.

Come Into My Life

The cartoon character, Charlie Brown, might say it this way, "To love me is to understand me."

If we expect to be understood, we must be willing to disclose ourselves. Let me describe, for example, what often happens when a wife feels her husband doesn't understand her. She becomes silent and sulky. Her moodiness confuses him, and he asks himself, "Now what have I done?" He is surprised when she expresses displeasure with him. His response is something like this, "How was I to know? You never told me how you felt about it." She, in turn, retorts angrily, "Well, you should have known!" If she really wanted him to understand, she should have shared her thoughts and feelings about the issues that disturbed her.

The failure to be self-disclosing is the primary cause of nearly all misunderstandings between husbands and wives. Each seems to feel that the other should telepathically sense or, as a diviner, magically discern unexpressed feelings and thoughts. Since they don't have these powers, they can't understand what hasn't been divulged. Hence, there is misunderstanding and conflict.

We don't freely disclose ourselves for two reasons. First, to be known is to be vulnerable. Generally, when I choose not to reveal something from my inner life it's because I view it as an embarrassment or a weakness. And, if someone wants to hurt me and knows about this secret part of my life, that person can easily do so by attacking it.

Here is how we use this tactic in interpersonal confrontations. If I know that the person with whom I am in conflict has a "skeleton" in his closet, I may choose to bring this hidden embarrassment to his attention. I gain some satisfaction from his painful struggle to emotionally deal with this past shameful behavior, now in the open.

Secondly, we confide our private selves with others only when we completely trust them. We trust those persons who have first proved that they genuinely love us. This love is the key that unlocks our minds and hearts and allows our hidden selves to fully emerge. Love accepts weakness in one another and responds with supportive understanding.

The ability to distinguish between thinking and feeling, and to appropriately respond to each, is another important skill we need if we are to understand another. Thinking understands thoughts and feeling understands feelings. Husbands and wives can't understand one another unless their communication flows appropriately through both thinking *and* feeling channels. Failure to learn and implement this principle of communication accounts for more breakdowns in love relationships than any other disruptive force.

Psychological research shows a distinct difference between men and women in ways of communicating. We know that the basic style of communication for 60 percent of males is thinking. Conversely, 60 percent of females communicate with feelings rather than with thoughts. When a "thinking" man and a "feeling" woman choose each other - which occurs in nearly two out of three marriages - faulty communication often leads to stormy and quarrelsome patterns of relating.

June and Chris

June had learned to love her husband, Chris, and accepted the person he chose "to be." But she continued to long for a deeper, emotional level of understanding with him. Chris is a "thinker." He works in a scientific profession that requires logical analysis and the practice of precision. June related how she often poured out her deepest feelings to Chris who patiently listened to her for a little while. Then, without rancor, he quietly left the house and went to his office. When he could not deal with their conflicts in a rational and objective manner, Chris physically removed himself. Rather than to try clumsily to identify with and share her heart's burden and relieve her tears, he left her alone to carry on a silent emotional monologue. She, of course, felt spurned by his refusal to understand the intensity of her feelings.

The scene was repeated when they were together with me in therapy. June disclosed her feelings about a sensitive issue, and I asked Chris how he *felt* about her disclosure. He replied, "Well, I *think* that..." When I pressed him to share his feelings rather than his thoughts, he became quiet and stared straight ahead. Although he could not physically withdraw, he could retreat into himself. At these times I felt genuine empathy for him, for I knew he was not resisting stubbornly. He was helpless and felt emotionally inadequate. Chris had never related with another person at deep feeling levels. But it was something that I felt he wanted to learn. He knew that he would not be able to truly understand his beloved until he was able to communicate with her through his feelings.

*   *   *

Love understands, and wants to know totally the one upon whom it showers its affections. Love seeks to understand before it insists on being understood. It says to the beloved, "Show me your most secret self, the one that you have never let any other person see. For only as I know you, will my understanding of you become whole."

167

Exercise

TIME FOR UNDERSTANDING

Select a concern that lays heavily on your heart and ask your husband to be your understanding confidant. Use as much time as you need to fully share your thoughts and feelings. Your husband will actively listen, reflecting on what he is hearing and asking you to explain more fully or to clarify anything that he doesn't understand. He will not give advice, offer answers or solutions, or attempt to correct what you say. He will convey his understanding by nodding his head, by reassuring smiles, and by comfortingly touching your hand.

When you feel you have been understood, reverse the process. You will be the confidante for your husband. If he has no concern to share at this time, he may choose to wait for another time to open his heart to you. In any case, let him know you are ready to listen when he needs to open his life to you.

Listening Times can be scheduled as frequently as needed, when one or both of you want to share your inner selves with the other. There is no greater joy in life than being understood by one who loves and cares.

CHAPTER TWELVE

Love's Bubblegum Effect

tempered by the trials of its labors,
love expands to carry its load

Discussing his growing love relationship, a twenty-two-year-old man said to me, "Oh yeah, that's love's bubblegum effect." He used this metaphor to show how love holds two people together when tensions threaten to break up their relationship. From the beginning of a relationship to its consummation in a love-bond, there are peaks and valleys, good times and bad times, and maybe some cheers followed by tears. But because a love-bond is uncommonly elastic, the strains placed upon it can be eased before a break occurs.

This "bubblegum effect" is love's capacity for long-suffering. Love doesn't relinquish its hold at the first moment it is abused or neglected. It bears injury and insult as part of building and maintaining a relationship. "Love suffers long."[1] It is tenacious and stubbornly resists uncoupling from the person with whom it is bonded.

Even when stretched to the breaking point, love wants to remain loyal to its beloved. The spirit of love is not easily conquered. Often rebuffed or spurned, it continues to give until the last glimmer of hope fades away.

169

At times, love loses its vigilance. It assumes that all is well in the relationship and then is unprepared to give when giving is needed. But love is also patient because it understands our weakness. When a loved one is distressed, love is gentle in its requests and offers assistance rather than makes demands. It senses when the loved one is struggling with feelings of disappointment. Love is aware when its beloved is tired and weary, depleted of emotional and physical energy. Likewise, love acknowledges that selfishness occasionally creeps into our lives and prevents us from loving. It is possible for love to grow weary in doing good deeds and to slumber. If love is laboring within me, I know well how it is also toiling in my wife. Therefore, when she takes a respite from loving, I understand. Love realizes that because of these and many other human weaknesses, love in another is temporarily subdued. When these human failings stand between a husband and wife, love's long-suffering holds the relationship together.

Stresses, problems, disappointments, fatigue, selfishness, and love's own weariness are naturally present in our human striving, and they easily foil our best intentions. Love can be derailed much like any other moving force in our life. When this happens to one individual in a love relationship, the other carries the love-load of two people. Withdrawal by one partner from the joint work of love is the signal for the other to labor alone until the co-laborer returns to love's work force.

Martha

The length of time one partner is required to do most of the loving varies from a few moments to many years. Martha, 41 years old, sought my help to resolve unexpected issues associated with her husband's recovery from alcoholism. She was the "co-dependent," or "enabler," who compensated for her husband's irresponsible behaviors. Carrying the burden of the relationship, Martha managed the home and raised their children with little help from him. She told me often that she wished her husband would be more considerate. He gave his love infrequently and sparingly. Although Martha's need for affection was rarely satisfied, she continued to give love to him. Some will argue that as an enabler she was meeting her own psychological and emotional needs through long-suffering. I learned during the course of her therapy, however, that she was truly in love with her husband.

In the early years of his recovery, he began again to contribute to their love-bond. Martha now rejoices in receiving love as well as in giving it, although her contributions are still given more graciously than are her husband's. The dream she held for so many years is becoming fulfilled because her love refused to succumb to the consequences of her husband's alcoholism. Love's "bubblegum effect" had done its work.

*   *   *

In Western cultures, egocentricity has replaced the love in love relationships. And its demand for immediate gratification undermines every relationship it rules. We have become a nation of people chasing after selfish interests.

Impatience is found everywhere in our society. We don't like to be kept waiting and we expect to receive things when

171

we want them, not when another chooses to give. We react angrily against those who seem to make us wait. Patient endurance without complaint, once an "old fashioned" virtue, has vanished. It shouldn't surprise us, then, that couples "in love" early find their relationships coming apart. The message that goes out from one or both, verbally and behaviorally, is "Love me; I need it, and I want it now."

If a wife senses that her husband is becoming less attentive, often she tries to revive it by claiming that he is inconsiderate. She may say, "You never take me anywhere anymore" or, "You never want to go along with me to see my family" or "You forgot our anniversary again." There are times when our love for each other must be aroused. Whimpering, grumbling, and complaining, do not, however, awaken love to action. Instead they create feelings of guilt and defensiveness that invite a counterattack.

This is where steadfast love, not a reprisal, should be brought to bear. Love from one spouse keeps communication channels open and helps the other bring his love back to their love-bond.

But, you say, "One person can't go on giving endlessly without love in return. There has to be a point where loving stops." And I agree. Many times it is futile for the love of one spouse to continue as a unilateral bond in a love relationship. This completely exhausts the person who gives but doesn't receive. Martha sometimes felt she had reached this point with her alcoholic husband. Prior to the beginning of his recovery, she said, "I don't know how much longer I can be responsible for the survival of both of us." It is possible to become so physically, emotionally, and spiritually drained that to cease loving is a wise choice.

Come Into My Life

Therapists must expose the self-deception that *givers* and *takers* use to conceal the real foundation for their relationships. Spouses who take reduce giving spouses to "means" for their "ends." This happens, however, only because the spouses serving as "means" give the other spouses permission to use them. And they allow themselves to be used as long as they consider their users *worthy* of their enabling gifts.

We value "ends" but dismiss "means" until we need them again. So, when "ends" lose their value, those serving as the "means" stop giving. In a relationship in which the wife, for example, gives and the husband takes, she in time runs out of gifts because his loveliness, which prompted her to give, has lost its compelling attraction. Her husband is left to deal with his frustration and with the pain of his wife's rejection. He rails against his wife from whom he had taken the indulging love. Removed from the center of her attention and deprived of gratification on request, he tries in every way to restore the old relationship that was built upon the inequities of a one-way love-bond. The efforts of two people were expended to benefit just one. This is not fair in a relationship in which two people profess to have a mutual love-bond.

One-way relationships develop during courtship as in marriage. A suitor, unhappy because he tried to give his love to a woman who wouldn't receive it, refused to be discouraged. Repeated rejections couldn't persuade him to abandon his quest for her love. This led to the question, "Is he in love or does his persistence indicate an emotional or psychological need that this particular woman fulfills in his life?" I concluded that it was the latter, because love doesn't seek or find pleasure in being injured. So, laying the relationship issue aside, we turned to the treatment of this emotional/psychological issue.

173

Love's Bubblegum Effect

Love withstands great pressure before breaking. But in our egocentric society, couples often surrender to the strains on their relationships long before love has had enough time to do its work. It's not surprising that fifty percent of divorced people who remarry say that they were better off the first time around.

Many couples are married long before the love-bond has been established. They marry when their love is in the "roller-coaster" stage, and they are still searching for loveliness in each other. During this get-acquainted time they learn to respect one another's personalities, interests, and behavioral patterns, although they may become irritated when these differences are exhibited. Collisions with each other become an uphill struggle in which their relationships merely chug along. Then, as the conflicts are resolved, they ride smoothly together downhill.

Courtships need to continue as long as needed for men and women to know each other. This time of testing determines if their loves can grow deeply enough to respond patiently and sensitively when they reveal their differences to one another. Their future relationship is at serious risk if they wait to do this after they have exchanged wedding vows. These new self-disclosures then evoke emotional reactions - surprise, confusion, and anger, and generally in this order. Because they haven't tested their professions of love through self-disclosure, they become annoyed and estranged when troublesome patterns of behavior surface. Then comes the question, "Where is the person I married?"

Couples wait until after marriage before completely revealing themselves because they feel self-disclosure is then less risky. They believe that being their true selves, even when offensive, is a *right* given by marriage. While marriage can't grant this right, a long-suffering bond of love can overcome

174

different and initially disturbing behaviors if the courtship has been long enough to give it time to develop.

Husbands and wives can't rely upon marriage to hold them together in a troubled relationship. Without a fully developed love-bond they won't try to understand the reason(s) for behaviors they don't like. When love is in its infancy stage they blame their conflicts on each other's headstrong refusal to change. The wife says, "I don't know why he has to be so bullheaded!" And the husband counters, "Stubbornness is her middle name!" This attack upon each other's unreasonable and unyielding attitude continues until I intervene. Each is convinced that, "I have been as patient and long suffering as anyone could ever be."

It is not a matter of wanting to be obstinate. All behaviors satisfy some need - personal, emotional, spiritual, or physical. Therefore, our behavior changes only when we eliminate or change our need, or if we can devise different and more appropriate behaviors to meet the need.

Husbands and wives can endure marital troubles if they accept them as nonpersonal. If they can interpret unkind words and behaviors as thoughtless attempts to meet needs, not as personal attacks, they lose much of their sting. I find that spouses don't necessarily intend to injure one another by what they say and do. When they become aware of the hurt that is inflicted by their careless handling of love, they become contrite and apologetic. So I help them understand that when their attacking behaviors trample over their love for one another, it doesn't mean the love-bond has broken. It only means that because a pressing personal need demands satisfaction, they have momentarily reinserted themselves in the center of their own lives. The love they confess for one another has become redirected towards the self.

So I treat unlovely behaviors in terms of the needs they fulfill. In the privacy of individual sessions we examined these behaviors by asking, "What does this behavior do for you?" The focus of therapy becomes a search into self to uncover the pressing need that gave rise to the behaviors. When this need is disclosed, the conflict that was centered in the relationship re-focuses in the self and loses force. This is the conflict they must resolve: "How can I fulfill my needs and love my mate at the same time?" Conflicts are resolved by coming to grips with unconscious needs that shape behaviors.

Individuals change behaviors only when they acknowledge the self-deception that directs them. Then they understand how subtly egocentric needs create motives that determine the way they behave. In some instances they eliminate their needs; in others they change them. Sometimes they find more acceptable ways to meet their needs. And by restoring the beloved to the center of their life, they regain harmony in their relationship. Using this love relationship approach in therapy, we rely on loving understanding. We don't rely on compromises and contracts so common in most marriage counseling.

Mark and Doris

When behavior fails to consider the needs and feelings of the one towards whom it is directed, as in this case with Mark and his wife Doris, tunnel vision develops and sets the relationship helplessly adrift. Mark, married for a second time, worked hard to finance the education of his children from his earlier marriage. Angered by his wife's lack of interest, he confronted her with the statement, "I have something I want to discuss with you." This seems harmless enough until we look at the setting in which it was spoken. Mark was sitting with arms folded, and his wife had just walked into the house after a day of exhausting work. She reacted to his curt announcement with tight lips and a chilling silence. He, in turn, verbally assaulted her for being non-responsive and non-cooperative. When I asked Doris why she remained passive, she said, "Why talk? He always has his mind made up about anything we talk about. Anything I say is not going to make any difference. This is the way it has always been."

At first, it appears that Mark is arbitrarily demanding and rigid. But not so. He is a professional man who rose to his present position from modest beginnings. His success came from self-discipline, self-denial and a well ordered and tightly managed lifestyle. Risks were minimized, *nothing was left to chance.*

Marks' inflexible approach to life reflects his insecurity. He doesn't have confidence in himself to overcome unexpected obstacles and demands in a new venture. So he tries to prepare for any contingency. He minimizes his anxieties by controlling the world around him. Doris was another aspect of his world that he expected to control. But she refused to yield to his hardened and insensitive control by passively resisting Mark's request for the "discussion." In this moment she didn't feel like his beloved wife. She felt more like an unruly child called upon to account for her failure to conform.

In our sessions, Mark and I talked at length about his personal insecurities which translated into a need for well organized plans with assured outcomes. His trust was in his plans and the sense of control they gave him. When his wife interfered with his plans, or refused to comply with them, Mark became anxious. And the fact that he couldn't make her feel equally anxious about his concerns irritated him more. He developed a stiff and business-like attitude with his wife.

Time and again Mark put her in the shadow of his urgent problems, but Doris could not feel his heightened level of concern. She didn't have his need for structure and guaranteed outcomes because she trusted herself - and Mark as well - to be able to handle problems as they came up.

Using the insights he gained from therapy, Mark began to develop less threatening behaviors to enlist his wife's cooperation. Now he knew that many of his behaviors were used to maintain the stability of a shaky self. With this understanding, I suggested to him that he use a "model statement" to communicate with his wife on sensitive issues: "Doris, when you have a little time, I have some thoughts about something that needs both of our attention. Maybe the two of us can come up with some kind of a solution." This helped him understand how the *soft approach*, even when he was anxious and unsettled, would more successfully elicit Doris' help to deal with a problem.

Doris, feeling more like his equal, then had no need to defend herself with passive defiance. She discussed problems with him to arrive at shared solutions, and Mark now considered her suggestions more seriously. But most of all, because she understood his lack of self-confidence, she accepted his behaviors nonpersonally when he slipped back into the "old ways." Love's "bubblegum effect" had performed successfully.

The patience and long-suffering of love enables husbands and wives to *compatibly disagree*. Love that stretches and then springs back into its original state of richness and fullness, allows two people to differ without putting their relationship at risk.

Exercise

STRETCHING YOUR LOVE-BOND

1. Select a behavior, an attitude, or mannerism of your spouse that you find disturbing.
   Example: "My wife always wants to do things on the spur of the moment."
2. Then, look within yourself and determine why you are upset by what your spouse is doing, how it interferes with your life. Write your answer(s) on paper.
   Example: "This is upsetting to me because:
   - a. it interferes with plans I have made,
   - b. I prefer to keep things planned ahead,
   - c. it doesn't give me enough time to prepare my attitude to enjoy what she wants to do, particularly if it happens to be something I don't like."
3. Try to establish what need(s) your spouse is fulfilling by this particular behavior.
   Again, record your answer(s) on paper.
   Example: "My wife does this because:
   - a. she just likes to live spontaneously,
   - b. she loses her enthusiasm when she is not immediately gratified,
   - c. it's her way of putting a little adventure into her life, i.e., doing things without planning."
4. In a considerate and loving way, share your findings with your spouse,
   noting: what need(s) you think your spouse is satisfying:
   Example: Discuss with your spouse your answers to number three (3),
   noting: how you feel your spouse's behavior, attitude, or mannerism hinders you from being the person you want to be:
   Example: Discuss with your spouse your answers to number (2).
5. From your sharing, agree on ways by which the tension on the love-bond can be reduced - by resolving differences related to the behavior, attitude, mannerism that you find annoying.

Example: You:
  a. try to anticipate things she may want to do so that they won't catch you by surprise,
  b. urge your wife to look ahead to things she may want to do and tell you in advance,
  c. keep your wife informed of your schedule so she will be aware of the inconvenience she will cause by her "spur of the moment" decisions,
  d. work on loosening up your life a little more, catch some of her adventurous spirit,
  e. try to remember that your love for your wife is the only attitude (c. under number 2) that enables you to gracefully share in her enjoyments,
  f. ask your wife to offer any suggestions she may have to reduce the tension on the love-bond.

Following this format, you will be applying *Love's Bubblegum Effect* to any conflict, lessening the tension on your long-suffering love-bond that is stretched by the differences in your personalities and preferences.

CHAPTER THIRTEEN

Rekindling A New Flame

love's intellect has 20/20 vision

Often a married couple, in love, examines its love-bond in later years and discovers that it is weak and ready to break. It no longer has the "bubblegum effect." The earlier romantic flame has lost its emotional glow. A few smoldering memories of ardor remain, but the husband and wife can't arouse the dying embers.

When romantic love has burned itself out, most couples try to revive flames of passion in the same way they started them initially. They expect to find the old spark, but they cannot. Disillusioned and resigned to failure, they lament, "We can't love each other the way we once did."

Taking our lessons from the daily afternoon "soaps," we have been told that "falling in love" is the only way to enter into a love relationship. Tales of romantic passion discourage us from exploring alternatives for restoring a burned out love. We wait for that magic emotional spark to start a new flame in our hearts.

In truth, a couple in this situation needs to ignite its love in a new way and refuel it with a different type of energy. The only match that can start a new flame in an old love comes from the mind's eye, not from the heart's beat. The fuel to keep it burning is the ongoing search for the lovely qualities in one's beloved. This leads to the discovery of a new and different kind of beauty: a beautiful person who is in the process of "becoming" and who desires another person to share and assist in that process.

Spouses in search of each other's beauty invite one another "to help me become more lovely." They are willing to unfold their inner selves so that each can know where the other desires to grow in loveliness and how to be part of that growth. When they have opened their lives to be seen and known, love for one another then comes from the understanding of the mind, not from the fickleness of a feeling.

Thus, they create a new love-bond that is emotionally rich and substantively real. Their love touches the cords of their intellects which *knows* the goodness of their spouse that makes him or her so lovely. The mind's knowledge then stirs the heart's feeling. Aroused feelings, in turn, inspire the mind to explore more deeply in order to know more completely. So love grows, and for the first time in the relationship it is not imprisoned by the rapture of emotions. Now when they say, "I love you," it is because they know the beauty in their beloved that has given birth to this love.

The fire of love burns again, more deliberately set, more carefully fueled with considerate and loving attending, and more controlled by open and sincere communication. It glows brightly through the years, because the eye of the mind never loses sight of the sparkling loveliness in the other.

In our daily social interactions we analyze other people's personalities and conclude that we like some, but not all of their traits and behaviors. We are pleased with the ways that we are similar. At the same time, if we want to relate with them, we have to adjust to the values, traits, and behaviors woven into their lives that we dislike and even find annoying. Relationships thrive because the similarities of the two parties are so satisfying that they neutralize the differences. Being different in some respects therefore, doesn't diminish the quality of their relations. If this is true in daily life, it is *most* true of relationships secured by the bond of patient, mutual love.

Many men and women, whose marriages have flattened out, adopt the wistful thinking of the pop song artist who sings, "Maybe the old song will bring back the old times." They feel if they can go back in time, they will find their old romance. But the most gratifying love is the love that is yet to be, not the love that has been. Shedding the passionate infatuations of the "old times," husbands and wives are free to enter into the enduring love that ushers in the "new times."

I have found time and again that a new flame of love can be rekindled in tired marriages. When they were willing to try, a husband and wife used their minds to build a new bond of love. They searched for the beauty in each other that their feelings had prevented them from seeing. In nearly every case these couples were delightfully surprised by what they had uncovered.

As a therapist, my perceptions of a husband and wife are not distorted by their confused feelings towards each other. So I rather quickly identify their beautiful personal qualities. My role is to lead them to explore these qualities in each other. Their perception of what I have discovered comes slowly. And in the beginning they are not all that enamored by my discoveries because their obstinate feelings still blur the richness of what they see. But when they do clearly discern them, they can't resist holding on to the beauty their minds behold.

183

Rich and Lynn

When Lynn came to me for help to resolve some marital conflicts, she had moved out of the house and was having an affair with a man whom she had met in her place of employment. She discovered in her "new flame" a tenderness and a capacity for emotional sharing missing in her husband, Rich. She tried to convince herself, and me, that the boyfriend provided a romantic love that Rich would not or could not give. Yet, Lynn couldn't understand why she was unable to decide to separate permanently from Rich. Her feelings urged her to say yes, but her thinking prevented her from yielding to this urge. For several sessions we wrestled with her vacillation. In time it became clear to both of us that she was focusing so intently on Rich's deficiencies that she couldn't see his beautiful side.

I learned from my sessions with Rich that he was a fine human being, esteemed by his employers and colleagues. And he was the same admirable person at home. He worked hard to maintain and improve the new house that he and Lynn had built. Since both were employed in full-time careers, Rich shared the homemaking activities with his wife. Because they had no children, Rich fully expected Lynn to pursue a life of personal and professional fulfillment. He was not abusive in any way. He kept physically fit with regular exercise and good eating habits, and he did not smoke, abuse alcohol or take illicit drugs. He was viewed by others as responsible and reliable.

I recognized quickly Rich's good qualities which Lynn couldn't see. Her objectivity was distorted by a selected way of looking at Rich that was mired in emotional turmoil and pain. Her need for romance blinded her mind's eye. She so completely focused on his failure to respond to her need for emo-

184

tional warmth and tenderness that she didn't see the many ways in which he was contributing to the richness of the other dimensions of her life.

Lynn wanted to communicate totally with Rich. He shared only his outer self, the same self he shared with friends and professional peers. Yearning to be more a part of him, she forgot his praiseworthy qualities which originally she had found attractive. She summed up her disappointment this way: "I resent Rich taking from the marriage what he wants and not giving me what I need."

Lynn and I studied Rich's personality, getting to understand him better. In times his wholeness began to emerge. She became more aware of his many good qualities that had faded with the rise of her emotional hurt. She compared these qualities with the elements that were missing from their relationship. The scales tipped in favor of the "good Rich." Lynn decided she had more to lose than to gain from terminating their marriage. They grew close, loving with the mind. Their hearts, *inspired by their intellects*, opened up to the tranquil love that flowed from their mind's discovery of each other's beauty.

Lynn learned that she could not write a description of an ideal husband and then find this "dream man" in real life. This is material for a fairy tale. Any person we choose to love has some personal and behavioral traits that do not appeal to us. However, husbands and wives can grow to be more of what each hopes to find in the other - if they love one another.

In many of my cases, one spouse or the other may feel it is futile to try to awaken their old love. He or she has looked for, and often found, another person with whom "to fall in love." For some, this search is repeated a second, a third, and even a fourth time. Either from despair or emotional exhaustion, they ultimately give up the quest for "true love." Their search always fails, because they look for a love where it can't be found, in the rise and fall of impassioned emotions. They insist on feeling love rather than *knowing* love. It is easier and more pleasant to fall into a love relationship than to climb up to the lofty peak of the "mind's love." This journey to love takes more time and effort, but it has a rewarding, permanent destination.

On the other hand, many couples choose to live together without a love-bond when their romantic flame has gone out. Togetherness, at least, satisfies their need for companionship. In these loveless relationships they elude loneliness.

For others, remaining in their relationships is an economic necessity. The standard of living and lifestyles they have worked hard to achieve can't be maintained from a single income. They pool their money but not their love.

In other cases, religious and moral values keep them together. A "humdrum" marriage is preferred to a guilt-ridden conscience.

Finally, many couples retain their marital alliance just so their children can be raised in a two-parent home.

Marriage fulfills all of these needs, but leaves husbands and wives chronically unhappy and feeling empty. Loveliness, clearly discerned by the searching mind, *alone*, effectively transforms the spiritless union of a man and woman in a mechanically contrived marriage into a spirit-filled relationship of loving togetherness.

Have you ever drawn up a list of your spouse's personal traits? Probably not. In our day-to-day relationship with each other, we find ourselves objecting to various habits and manners. But we fail to recognize all that is good and lovely. Taking them for granted, we don't tell our mates how much we admire

186

them for the beautiful parts of their personalities. Other people readily observe and praise the wonderful things that we ignore in one another. We, instead, routinely and selectively note and censure those traits that we don't like in our spouse.

In the activity that follows you will have an opportunity to deliberate on your mate's loveliness. I think you will be pleasantly surprised to learn that you are married to a beautiful person. I have structured the exercise to tap your thinking, not your feelings. When you have come *to know* your beloved, pass that knowledge along to your heart where the warmth of love will set it aglow.

Exercise

KNOWING YOUR BELOVED

This exercise lists 21 personal traits. Each trait includes descriptive statements that define it. The traits are measured from a 5 on the left to a 1 on the right. The numbers are equated as follow: five (5) = 100% of the time, four (4) = 80% of the time, three (3) = 60% of the time, two (2) = 40% of the time, and one (1) = 20% of the time. After reading the interpretive sketch for each trait, determine the frequency with which you feel it applies to your spouse.

Do not plan to complete your assessment in a single setting. Deliberate on each trait until you feel confident that your selection honestly reflects your best judgment. When both of you have completed your appraisals, choose a quiet and unhurried time when you can sit down and lovingly share them with each other. You may want to use several sessions - in relaxing moments at home, driving along in your automobile, over a dinner in a restaurant, etc. - to explore one another's personalities and behaviors in greater depth. As you discuss the traits, cite situations and events which you have used to guide you in your decisions.

187

Each of you should then decide how you want to use this newly discovered personal data to help you grow in loveliness. Suggest ways that you can assist one another in your journeys to a higher level of beauty.

Remember, some of these traits are more lovely when expressed in the moderate range than at the extremes. Prudence is perhaps the most beautiful virtue of all.

Considerate   5   4   3   2   1

My beloved is thoughtful about the effects of words and behaviors on others, doesn't use others as stepping stones, doesn't selfishly pursue personal goals at the expense of others.

Flexible   5   4   3   2   1

My beloved adjusts to changes rather than fights them, adapts to different types of people, yields to reasonable influence and persuasion, is not known for being headstrong, doesn't hold to views at any cost.

Interesting   5   4   3   2   1

My beloved is a fascinating person, attracts others with charming qualities, is able to hold the attention of others, could not be accused of being dull and boring.

Self-Dependent   5   4   3   2   1

My beloved looks inside of self for resources when things become difficult, is self-reliant, believes the adage "when things get tough the tough get going," isn't afraid to attempt things alone.

Industrious   5   4   3   2   1

My beloved is hard working, diligently attends to tasks until finished, is there when duty calls, doesn't use fatigue as an excuse to avoid work, doesn't wish for things but works for them.

Sensible   5   4   3   2   1

My beloved has good judgment about things, uses foresight not hindsight, is on target with common sense in most situations, doesn't do

Come Into My Life

foolish things before thinking, doesn't act before knowing outcomes of actions.

Faithful   5   4   3   2   1
My beloved is unwaveringly loyal to commitments, scrupulously honors promises, is a "true blue" spouse, would never betray the trust of others, doesn't need a contract to bind her/him to an agreement.

Open   5   4   3   2   1
My beloved unfolds the inner self through behaviors and words, wears the "real self" on the outside, is not guarded, doesn't conceal thoughts and feelings to hide the self from others.

Trustful   5   4   3   2   1
My beloved is willing to take risks with people, is not suspicious and skeptical of others' motives, doesn't interact with others with doubt and misgiving - looking for signs of insincerity and deception.

Responsible   5   4   3   2   1
My beloved lives by the motto "count on me," doesn't arbitrarily ignore expected behaviors, is not distracted from tasks by slothfulness and self-indulgence, is personally answerable to obligations and commitments.

Altruistic   5   4   3   2   1
My beloved is compassionate, brings comfort and solace to others, is unselfishly devoted to those in need, is not indifferent to the pain and suffering of others.

Venturesome   5   4   3   2   1
My beloved likes to try new things, experiments with new ideas, takes reasonable chances, doesn't need the guarantee of success before starting a task/project.

Emotional   5   4   3   2   1
My beloved appropriately expresses the normal range of feelings -joy, enthusiasm, fear, frustration, irritation, etc. - doesn't always pass feelings through the mind for approval, is not always serious and formal.

Self-Believing   5   4   3   2   1

My beloved appreciates the self, enjoys being alone with self, accepts personal weaknesses and strengths, feels able and competent, doesn't react defensively to criticism, can say "I like me."

Cheerful   5   4   3   2   1

My beloved is lively, a "breath of fresh air" that buoys the spirits of others, sees each day as sunny, is high-spirited, is not moody, doesn't go around looking glum.

Calm   5   4   3   2   1

My beloved has thoughts and feelings under control, handles the unexpected with composure, is not easily ruffled, is seldom caught in the middle of a heated argument.

Optimistic   5   4   3   2   1

My beloved looks on the bright side of things, approaches life with a "can do" attitude, is a "cheerleader" in the group, sees a "glass half-full" not "half-empty," is not discouraged by setbacks.

Sensitive   5   4   3   2   1

My beloved is aware when others' feelings are injured, is affected by emotional or physical pain of others, would not share in an activity that would hurt another.

Active   5   4   3   2   1

My beloved believes life is for the living, is energetic, guides life with the catch words "go" and "do," is a "shaker and mover," is not easily fatigued, is seldom idle.

Patient   5   4   3   2   1

My beloved can endure disappointments without complaint, doesn't react angrily when things don't go as expected, doesn't become restless with delay, doesn't give up when things go wrong.

Sociable   5   4   3   2   1

My beloved is neighborly and friendly, is approachable and companion-able, mixes well in the crowd, is not hostile and combative, doesn't alienate others, is not a fault-finder creating defensiveness in others.

CHAPTER FOURTEEN

Love Relationship Therapy

healing broken love in marriage

Love relationship therapy is not complex. Unlike most counseling theories, it doesn't have its own cumbersome nomenclature. I have been careful not to clutter up the emotional richness of a *relational therapy* with intellectual terms that constantly shift the process from feeling to thinking. At the same time, both therapist and patient relate through emotional feelings that flow between and within them. Their feelings don't escape the mind's grasp.

Every counseling system has some structure. But I have avoided shaping love relationship therapy into a rigid process that inhibits the natural interaction of therapist and patient along paths that are most appropriate at any moment. Love relationship therapy is not a recipe found in a standard cookbook of therapeutic theories. Rather, it is a set of principles that allows the therapist to be creative and to guide the intuitive leading of two human spirits in service to one person.

Further, there is little need to preplan for the therapy hour. I trust my patients to know which feelings and issues we will process in the short time we have together. This is particularly so when we analyze the "love" in their love relationship. When they tell me what changes they want to make in their lives, and in their relationship, I help them explore the personal, emotional, and psychological dynamics that stand in the way. I bring my professional expertise in the clinical analysis of these behavioral forces to our personal and spiritual encounter.

But the special gift I bring to the relationship is *me* and not the carefully crafted persona of the professional therapist. I am not the detached analyst, dissecting the problems and lives of feuding spouses. Instead, I am the caring therapist, with all of my humanness, whom my patients have asked, "Will you come into our lives?" I do not take the invitation lightly. I am privileged to be trusted to keep the confidence of all the intimacies they share with me.

Over the years I have learned that people who ask me to be their therapist want me to be part of their struggle with those problems and conflicts within the larger challenge of life we all confront daily - finding relief from loneliness. They don't expect me to solve their problems and resolve their conflicts. They are too embarrassed to ask me what they really want: "Please accept me. Know me. Understand me." Yes, they have family and friends who could be their confidants, but they, too, are shut inside their own lives - alone without the awareness of loneliness.

The therapist's love for his patients is the key to successful outcomes. Attracted by the loveliness that I discern in the lives of the husband and wife who unfold themselves to me, I dispense the love I prescribe. Their puzzled expressions tell me that my loving attentiveness confuses them. They came into therapy expecting a counselor who will grapple with their problems, and they find a person whose spirit of love and concern touches their spirits.

Come Into My Life

I know we are in touch with each other by what they say. "You're really investing in me." "Why are you doing this (going well beyond the allotted hour) for me?" "I feel close to you." These responses tell me that they aren't accustomed to unconditional love, that they have an emotional void to be filled, and that they doubt their loveliness. In turn, they know I have accepted the invitation to fully come into their lives.

Getting Started

In 80 percent of cases the call for help comes from the wife. Generally it is simple and direct, "My name is... A friend of mine that you had in therapy told me you would be able to help me with my marriage." She then elaborates on the estranged relationship with her husband. When she has completed her "story," I use the next few minutes to gather some basic intake information - address, phone number, years married, children, duration of the conflicts, and history of any previous counseling.

In the first session with the husband and wife I begin to weave my way into their life setting. Their conflicts have come out of that setting. I need to understand it because they are captives within it.

I ask them about their jobs, their children, their siblings, their birth positions, their parents, their parents' work, their parents' marital relationships, their leisure activities and hobbies, their pets, their house, their family routines, their relationship with each other's parents, their religious faith and church affiliation, and anything else I can think of. If after this first session we decide to work together, I request pictures of their children, parents, and other significant people in their lives. I am not comfortable working with faceless people. What I don't get to see in real life or in pictures I see in the mental images I create. It is important that I move with them in their world. I make their experiences my experiences. I am, after all, a guest in their lives.

Doing the personal inventory at the outset serves two purposes: 1) it opens the door for me to enter their lives, and 2) it reduces their initial anxiety while we are getting acquainted.

Therapy continues with their presentations of the "problem." It is not easy for them to be as open and candid as I want them to be. Each presents his/her "case" fully aware that the other may interrupt with emotional encounters. While they talk I listen. Reassuringly, I let them know, "I understand. I am with you."

With their heavy feelings lifted, they anticipate my reactions. But silence follows, and they quizzically stare at me. During the silence I hear the question they don't ask: "Well, what are *you* going to do about it?"

I don't answer that question. Instead, I ask both of them, "Do you love your husband/wife?" They aren't prepared for this question, and they stumble through their answers. In most cases it is "yes," but usually with qualifications. My reaction is pointed, "Your love doesn't seem to be working very well. The unlovely behaviors which you attribute to each other suggests that it is asleep on the job. Love doesn't say the things or act the way you have described."

I purposely create this opportunity to structure our relationship by distinguishing between "marriage counseling," which they expect, and "love relationship therapy," which I provide. At this time I make it clear that they are personally important to me and that I care very much about what is happening to them.

194

Come Into My Life

In my description of love relationship therapy, in contrast to marriage counseling, I include much of the material in this book, especially chapters one, two, and five. This leads us into a discussion of love that raises many questions and provides few answers. This, too, is by design. It whets their appetites and prepares the way for my invitation: "I can help you if you are willing to deal with your relationship as a problem in loving. But I can't help if you only want counseling for marital conflicts, which even when resolved won't help you love one another any more than you do now."

If they commit themselves to love relationship therapy, I dedicate myself to helping them kindle a new love for one another. With our relationship solidly established, we forge ahead to solve love's riddle, taking love from the poet's pen to actively direct the lives of a man and woman in love.

THE NEW PARADIGM OF HUMAN RELATIONSHIPS

Married couples are deeply affected with the concept of a love relationship when they understand how it exalts them, and how it towers over all other human relationships. So in our first sessions, they learn the new model of human relationships I have developed (chapters three and four).

Earlier in my practice I used this material only when needed to explain some aspect of love-relating that a spouse did not understand. The issue we discussed became clearer when we contrasted it to the other relationship bonds. However, this procedure detracted from our smooth therapeutic movement. Often it required a rapid change from emotional to intellectual considerations. The emotional energy directed toward those deep feelings was lost in this process.

I present the entire range of human relationships before analyzing the love in their relationship. I often use overhead transparencies that combine visual images with explanations of the relationship concepts. Because abstract concepts are confusing, these graphics help them conceptualize the complexities of human relating.

They must understand a love-bonded relationship before they can expect to achieve it. Through these visual symbols, couples see clearly that the love-bond is only one of several types of interpersonal relationship constructs.

A transparency serves several teaching purposes. Visual representations of the dynamics in relationships clarify the conflicts spouses encounter. They can then deal with those conflicts through reasoning instead of becoming lost in their heated emotions. In this way they explore the causes of their conflicts rather than attack one another's behaviors.

Secondly, the transparencies present a digest of the total range of human relationships which I can use as a reference to clarify issues. Patients easily identify a specific relationship issue by turning to the graphic illustrations which they have mentally imprinted. For example, when assessing their growth in love, they can refer to the image of the overlap of their lives and their life spaces, in the love-bonded relationship. We use the overlap to determine the extent of "two becoming one." Thus, we quickly and clearly process a relationship issue. (See Figure V, Chapter III.)

Most importantly, the graphics set the stage for the "playing out" of the love theme in their relationship. While viewing the transparencies we discuss the distinctive characteristics of love-bonded relating, contrasting them to the work of two people who are merely building a compatible marriage. Don't mistake the goal of therapy. *It is growth in love, not compatibility in relating.* Whereas love always assures "harmonious and loving togetherness," a compatible marriage need not have either love or even personal caring.

Using visual aids to initiate love-relationship therapy, following the initial sessions during which complaints are heard and conflicts are identified, serves three additional purposes. It eases an anxious couple gently into therapy which it does not understand and about which it often feels distrustful. Second, it moves one or both spouses from the "heat of emotions" to a rational and objective examination of their relationship. Third, it gives me control of the spouses' volatility in the early sessions. In brief, the visual aids show where we are going, how we plan to get there, and when we have arrived.

I provide husbands and wives ample opportunity to explore the demands of a commitment to the development of a love-bond.

ANALYZING THEIR LOVE

It isn't pleasant to have our behaviors towards our spouses measured by the yardstick of love. We sense that they will be found wanting, because behaviors seldom equal the measure of professed love.

Penetrating the defenses of a husband or wife, I make them vulnerable to the "I told you so" that one is tempted to inject into the discussion when the other admits a fault. Such an admission is embarrassing enough without the subsequent scorn of a spouse. We avoid this uncomfortable situation and create an environment for honest introspection by conducting the analyses of their loves in individual sessions. They feel free to be truthful, and I am free to be confrontive. They can leave their sessions reflecting on what was said and felt, and without feeling guilty.

Throughout this section I will discuss the analysis of love with the husband as patient. But all that I write here applies equally to the wife.

A husband won't change his behaviors while simultaneously defending his self-esteem. He doesn't choose to change simply because his wife has protested his behaviors. He changes only when he is convinced that "I ought to be different from the way I am."

When dealing with his behaviors in a love relationship, therefore, we judge them by an absolute and indisputable standard - love. Behaviors are defined as right or wrong by the *morality of love*.

In the first session I ask the husband what he thinks is wrong with their relationship. The answer nearly always focuses on his wife: "She is...and on...and on." Unwilling to answer forthrightly, he vindicates himself and blames his wife for the breakdown. But I persist, "I'm sure your wife has many failures that she needs to deal with, but let's talk about what you are doing that contributes to your conflicts. Maybe we can start by looking at her complaints about your behaviors. (The types of faults that spouses find in one another are listed in Chapter V). According to your wife, how should you be different from the person you now are?" He easily recalls the many behaviors that his wife constantly calls to his attention, as if they were on a mental tape that doesn't stop playing.

Come Into My Life

Although I have usually heard these complaints in sessions with his wife, I don't mention them to him for two reasons: 1) guarding confidentiality, and 2) protecting therapist-patient trust, without which there cannot be a therapeutic relationship. But more importantly, when they come from the husband I know they are disturbing him. He can't escape their nagging censure that leaves him disappointed with himself.

I challenge him on the loveliness of these behaviors, whether provoked or not. He tries to justify them, but his defense is weak because his conviction of his "rightness" is weak. They seldom meet love's criteria as described throughout this book, particularly as described in the closing paragraphs of the *Introduction*.

At this point, I do not press the issue of his failure to be loving towards his wife. It is more important that he understands how unlovingly he is behaving towards himself. An effective technique to start this area of therapy is the unexpected "shock" question, "Why don't you like yourself?" Generally, he has a puzzled look and replies, "What do you mean? I like myself."

My response is just as swift, "But I don't see that you are showing love for yourself through these behaviors. What do they do for you?"

His answers are evasive, "I have a right to do what I am doing if she's going to act the way she does." Or, "She wants me to be someone I'm not." Or, "I'll carry out my end of the bargain when she carries out her end."

I continue to beg the question. "You aren't receiving the rewards of love - a personal, spiritual, or emotional uplift - from the way you are relating. In fact you end up feeling discouraged and cast down. *The return on your behaviors is pain.*"

Together we uncover the pain he is experiencing but not acknowledging. He is sharing in a *sour relationship* marked by

199

snarls and scowls, without smiles and cheers. He feels alone even in the presence of his wife, having fallen out of favor with her. He is distressed and discouraged but doesn't know why. His disquieting guilt alienates him from himself - a loss of self-friendship. His home life lacks warmth and is chilled by inter-personal tensions. He feels inadequate and irresponsible as a husband. He is sexually unfulfilled because conjugal love is a casualty of their withering relationship. He is frozen in time, going nowhere.

Essentially, his relationship behaviors are self-punitive. And in other areas of his life we find more behaviors through which he unintentionally hurts himself. Perhaps he eats too much, or works too long and hard, or drinks excessively, or smokes, or fails to stay physically fit. (See the exercise at the end of Chapter Six for a longer list of ways we harm our lives by pursuing selfish desires and needs).

He is surprised that I interpret his behaviors to mean that he doesn't value himself. Yet, it is an axiom that we judge the worth of people by the way we treat them. He is abusing himself through his behaviors, thereby devaluing the person he says he loves. With this insight guiding our therapy, I urge him to direct more love toward himself. Until he becomes self-loving it isn't reasonable to expect him to treat his wife with love.

A caution is in order here. Writing an instructional manual for any procedure is easy. But using those instructions to complete the procedure usually takes great patience, especially when the procedure involves a variable with its own will - a human being. All of us have acted contrary to the wishes of others. We fail to follow their plan. And so the husband hears what we are discussing, but is not ready to comply with the message he has heard.

Come Into My Life

Moving from the acceptance of an insight to making the appropriate behavioral change is a big challenge. Despite recognizing the faults in the ways he relates to his wife, he steadfastly clings to his self-defeating behaviors for several reasons. First, the concept of self-love seems socially unacceptable - only vain people love themselves. I meet this argument with a discussion of the difference between *healthy* self-love and a narcissistic personality. Rightly assessing our worth and giving ourselves the love we merit, is not only socially acceptable but is morally required. This is very clear in Christian teachings. We are expected to love everyone, and this includes love *for* ourselves.

Secondly, he argues that he does love himself, and that his behaviors are self-defeating only because his wife is unreasonable. I counter this resistance by showing how his behaviors may be sowing the seeds of her attitudes towards him. Unloveliness evokes unloveliness. The *child* in us glosses over this truth by blaming others for the way we act. And so, in a very real sense, he is saying, "She made me do it."

Thirdly, the strength of egocentricity has to be broken. It is found in such expressions as: "That's the way *I* am;" or "*I* have always been this way;" "*I* don't see why *I* should change;" "Why can't she just accept me the way *I* am;" "She knew *I* was this way before we got married." He sees nothing wrong with living in the center of his own life. And his statements make sense as long as their basic premise isn't challenged. But I challenge it. I say to him, "You don't want your wife to love you. You want her to indulge you." He has equated love with indulgence. The message in his behaviors is, "Yield to my wishes." So he must decide if he wants to be in love with his wife or in love with himself. If it is with his wife, egocentric-bonding must be replaced with love-bonding.

A fourth, and the most difficult resistance to overcome is his feeling that he is unworthy and deserves the hurt he receives from his relationship, and from life in general. This feeling is deeply rooted in the unconscious self-concept. Because the self-concept is negative, he doesn't allow himself to consciously acknowledge it.

The denial of self-worth results ultimately in self-rejection. So we proceed slowly to determine the depth of his low self-valuation. This process usually requires some psychological probing and analysis of his earlier developmental life. I work gently during this search into his past and pause to wade through emotional pains from his recall of unresolved child and adolescent abuse or neglect.

His feelings about himself have been shaped by how he has perceived treatment from his significant others - parents or guardians. If he was treated unlovingly, he assumed he was unlovely. Or, if pampered and indulged, he concluded he was helpless and dependent. The child with low self-regard became the adult with low self-regard. So when bad things happen to him, consciously he resents the unfairness of his treatment. Unconsciously, he feels the unworthy person that he is deserves this hurt. Because he's not really as unworthy as he imagines, we work to build a new positive self-concept that better represents the worthy person he is.

Although he gradually acknowledges that his unlovely behaviors come back to him in the form of personal hurt, indicating a lack of self-love, he can't improve his self-image until he begins to relate with his wife in ways that make him feel good about himself. And so we discuss how to make these relationship changes. Here we evaluate his interactions with his wife, using love's criteria (chapters seven through thirteen.) The more these relationship behaviors satisfy the criteria, the more positive the feedback he receives from his *works of love*. In turn, he likes himself better and loves more.

But the process is not yet complete. For he must also feel comfortable *being loved*. Generally no strong emotions arise within us from the indulgence we customarily receive from our spouse. Love, however, arouses emotions in a way that indulgence cannot.

My wife may gratify my needs, comply with my wishes, please me, and even "spoil" me, and I accept these indulgences without the slightest prickling of emotions. Living in the center of myself, I expect them, even feel I deserve them. And my wife is obligated to provide them. This indulgence conceals how little I love myself. But with more love for myself and giving more love to my wife, I no longer need her indulgence to affirm my worth.

Affection and desire are awakened within me when she now gives *herself* to me with warmth, tenderness, and sweetness. Unfamiliar with these emotions, I don't know how to embrace her loving devotion. I find myself reflecting on the question. "Do I deserve her love?"

This is what love does. It humbles you, makes you conscious of self and makes you face your false pride and pseudo self-importance. But herein lies your loveliness. All arrogance is gone. You become soft-spoken. Modesty replaces vanity. Jesus recognized and gave this loveliness his greatest gift - "Blessed are the poor in spirit for their's is the kingdom of Heaven."[1] So the husband is both lovely and deserves love. And even as he gives, he must also receive.

THE WORK OF THE THERAPIST

The goal of love relationship therapy is to help a couple "grow in love." Love is something they know exists but have difficulty describing, much less practicing. Assisting a husband and wife to form a compelling vision of love, and of what they want in their relationship is the major role of the therapist. I am no more effective than my ability to lead them in a search for this vision.

Although I rely on husbands and wives to articulate their own images of love, I try to be the vision of loveliness they describe. My relationship with them serves as a guide to what they would like their relationship to become. With compassionate understanding and acceptance, I model the type of relationship they can have with one another. My embodiment of love *pulls* them along in their growth of love. It attracts and energizes them to move forward on their own without the push and pressure of my urgent appeals.

They must own this vision, knowing that it grows out of their needs. Thus, I draw on their spiritual and emotional resources to give it life. If they are committed to the vision, they will be less likely to resist when they reach the steepest part of the uphill climb - when they start asking, "Is it worth it?"

I learn from each couple I work with the hardships they encounter in their change from living for self to living for the other. In a symbiotic way I experience their struggles. Feeling their earnest desire to be successful in loving, I understand their frustrations with the slow pace. I know their disappointment when they slip back into the "old ways." But because I am *one* with them, they don't abandon the quest.

Come Into My Life

I must earn their support, not expect it because of my professional background. My influence must come only from my skill to lovingly attend to their patient efforts to place one another in the center of their lives. I create an atmosphere of trust which is the emotional adhesive binding me to the couple in their quest for love.

With the vision in front of them, the hard work begins - attaining it. They look to me for the impetus to move ahead. They have been locked for many years in a rigid routine of relating selfishly. Now, they expect me to commit them to action and to enable them to be agents of their own change. This is where the "art" of therapy empowers them and evokes their confidence and mastery in unfolding their love for self and for the other. And I must do this without taking control and responsibility for that process. For if I do, their development will be arrested. I help to build their self-confidence to manage their relationship, to find their roles and fulfill them. I am the "coach in the huddle," the "cheerleader on the sidelines," and the "referee on the field," but they are the players in the most important contest in their lives - growing in loveliness and in love.

The most trying task of the therapist is keeping the husband and wife committed to the goal and achieving it in small, almost imperceptible, steps. While they trudge along with only these minor changes as rewards for their efforts, many of their old behaviors persist. So, often they come to therapy sessions with a prepared agenda of problems and conflicts they want to deal with. The therapist must not allow himself to be sidetracked by the urgency of those concerns.

I use two strategies to keep the focus on the goal. First, we resolve the problem/conflict by relating it to the appropriate

205

member(s) of the "love team." In this way we use it as a stepping stone to achieve the over-arching goal of our therapy - growth in loveliness and loving. Second, I tell them early in therapy, the difficulties they can expect. One of these difficulties is, of course, learning to persevere without immediate gratification. Here is where I give the reassurance of a coach and the morale boost of a cheerleader. Using these therapeutic techniques, we defuse conflicts and hold to the basic purpose to which we are pledged.

Resistance many times becomes stubborn when we are required to move from the known to the unknown. A husband and wife may not be happy with their relationship, but at least they understand it and know what they can expect from it. But when they set out to achieve a new relationship, questions arise which they do not verbalize. Yet, I sense their cautions: "Is it really as lovely as it is pictured to be? Can we achieve it? Will we be able to keep it if we do achieve it? How much individual freedom will we be required to give up? And, aren't we opening ourselves to more emotional hurt when we lay down our defensive armor?"

Here, I call on their trust in me. I have seen the power of love at work. They have not. So I stay the course. I don't become caught up in their doubts and suspicions. I know that just a little further along is another success that warms their heart and deepens their hope. And we move on.

EPILOGUE

It has been more than a year since I completed the major portion of this book. During this time I have been applying the constructs of the love relationship system in marital therapy to the exclusion of all other counseling theories and models. You ask me, "Does it work?" My answer is, "Yes, if you trust love to perform its spiritual function, even when the personal and physical forces against it seem overwhelming." This is the central theme of the Christian message, "Love wins. It won't be conquered. Love is God, and God cannot be defeated."

Love relationship therapy is not an untested postulate. It is a principle of relationship bonding that has been proven in practice. For more than a year now, I have been working with a professional couple in a marriage that was on the brink of collapse. They have stabilized their marriage and have developed and strengthened a bond of love that is refreshingly new to their relationship. In the session I just concluded with the husband, and prompted me to sit down and write these final statements, we discussed how he is growing *out of self and into love with his wife.*

He talked about his youth and being "catered to by my parents." Life was easy for him, and he acknowledged that his parents had spoiled him. Meditatively he said, "I grew up doing what was good for me. It was easy for me to take the path of least resistance. When people our age got married, subconsciously we held on to the old habits of doing what was best

207

for ourselves. The old habits don't go away. It's hard to think of someone else before thinking of yourself."

It's relatively easy to change a behavior. *It's hard* to change a life. This man's life changed because he learned to appreciate the good person that he is. His introspection brought him face-to-face with unlovely behaviors and attitudes that detracted from the quality of his character. Constantly nudged by one of the several themes of our therapy, "Love is not attracted to unloveliness," he worked hard to become the type of person to which love is drawn. *He came to love himself without being in love with himself.*

Feeling secure in his own goodness, he no longer needed to make his desires/needs the centerpiece of his life. Gradually, he placed his wife in the vacancy which was created by the removal of himself.

He has overcome the major stumbling block to his love relationship. He is now growing in love with his wife, using the total team of love skills. For every problem, conflict, or issue that comes up there is a *love tool which he can use to resolve it.* He is becoming a skilled lover in the purest and noblest meaning of the word.

His wife went through the same "developmental love process." She, like her husband, now knows the frailty of a marriage covenant, and how easily it can crumble under the weight of the selfishness of the two people it holds together. And she, too, is learning to trust the strength of a love that has its center in the life of her husband.

Interestingly, when two people are united by a love-bond, they are then free to relate to one another using any of the other bondings. With love, each allows the self to be used by the other (egocentric), knowing that he/she will never be misused. With

208

love, each comes to the need of the other when he/she cannot provide for self (altruistic). With love, each becomes the other's best friend, sharing in one another's life and activities (personal). They now live with each other within the total range of relationships - even allowing each other the privacy of intrapersonal relating.

Come Into My Life

NOTES

Introduction

1. Aaron Beck has boldly printed the message that marriage counselors practice - love alone cannot sustain a marriage. But the fault lay not in love, but in the shallow description that he gives of love. The reader is referred to Aaron T. Beck, *Love is Never Enough*, (Harper and Row publishers, New York, 1988), pp. 185-189.
2. Epistle of I John 4:7, The King James Version of the New Testament.

Chapter I

1. The statistical profile from the census bureau notes that in 1991 30% of families were "married couples without children at home," and 26% of families were "married couples with at least one child under 18 living at home." At the same time unmarried couples increased from 523,000 in 1970 to 3 million in 1991. (Quoted in Parade Magazine, November 22 1992, p.16.)
2. Anthropologist Margaret Mead, who spent her life studying societies and cultures amorally, is noted for her intemperate suggestion that couples be joined by five-year renewable marriage contracts.
3. Stephen and Susan Schultz, *Marriage Joins Two People in the Circle of its Love*, (Blue Mountain Arts, Boulder, Colorado 80306.) Used by special permission.
4. In the chapter, *Rekindling a New Flame*, the reader is introduced to the process through which a lost love can be recaptured.

Chapter II

1. *Psychology Today*, February 1988, p.9
2. Ibid., p. 14
3. Ibid., p. 44
4. Ibid., p. 22
5. *Behavior Today Newsletter*, (ATCOM, Inc., 2315 Broadway, New York 10024.)
6. The reader can gain a better understanding of the italicized terms in these two paragraphs by reading Salvador Menuchin and H. Charles Fishman, *Family Therapy Techniques* (Cambridge, Massachusetts, Harvard University Press, 1981,) and Salvador Minuchin, *Families and Family Therapy* (Cambridge, Massachusetts, Harvard University 1974.) Minuchin is the father of the family therapy system and is liberally quoted and widely practiced.
7. I Cor. 13:5, The King James Version of the New Testament.

Chapter III

1. Quehl, Gary H., "A Report to the Campus," Council for Advancement and Support of Education, (Suite 400, 11 Dupont Circle, Washington, D.C. 20036), p. 27.
2. 1 Samuel 20:17, The King James Version of the New Testament.

Chapter V

1. Foreman, Robert F., "Lovesickness, A Way of Thinking About Substance Abuse and Dependence," *The Addiction*, a bi-monthly newsletter about substance abuse, (Alvernia College, Reading, Pennsylvania 19607), volume 1, Numbers 3 and 4, February and May, 1985.
2. Kernberg, Otto, interviewed by Linda Wolfe, "Why Some People Can't Love," *Psychology Today*, June 1978, p.59.
3. Aldridge, John, W., Professor of English, University of Michigan, "In the Country of the Young" *Harpers Magazine*, (October 1969), pp. 49-64, (November 1969), pp. 93-107.
4. Ibid, p. 49
5. Ibid, p. 50
6. Ibid, p. 50
7. Ibid, p. 53
8. Ibid, p. 104
9. Ibid, p. 103
10. In the chapter, "Love of Me Before Love of You," I discuss how individual psychological needs direct the flow of love in relationships. I have dealt separately with psychological need as a barrier because it is more of an unconscious factor than either the insistence on romance or the placing of self first in the relationship.

Chapter VI

1. Matthew 19:19, The King James Version of the New Testament.

Chapter VIII

1. 1 Cor. 13:5, The King James Version of the New Testament.

Chapter IX

1. Used by special permission of the Universal Press Syndicate.
2. Used by special permission of the author.

Chapter XII

1. 1 Cor. 13:4, The King James Version of the New Testament.

Chapter XIV

1. Matthew 5:3, The King James Version of the New Testament.

About the Author . . .

H. Dale Zimmerman

Dr. H. Dale Zimmerman approaches the subject of his book with the authority of nearly 40 years as a pastor, (Church of the Brethren) counselor, educator, and consultant, interacting with and touching the lives of many hundreds of individuals, couples and families. From this vast experience, he has tested traditional marriage counseling practices and found them to be wanting and deficient in most cases, offering a temporary and partial solution in others. The problem with conventional marriage counseling, Dr. Zimmerman has discovered, is the near-total absence of love as a therapeutic remedy. He shows clearly that this counseling offers "band aid" treatment instead of rebuilding a lasting foundation of mutual love in marriage.

Dr. Dale Zimmerman is Professor of Counseling and Human Services at Kutztown University of Pennsylvania and formerly served as Chairperson of the Department of Counseling and Psychological Services.

Over the past fifteen years, he has supervised more than forty professional counselors.

Dr. Zimmerman has directed The Psychological Alliance for Human Services, his own private counseling agency, for several years. Therapists associated with his agency provide marital relationship therapy and individual psychotherapy for a wide range of personal and psychological needs.

A prolific speaker, retreat leader, and workshop presenter, he has been a member of sixteen professional and psychological boards and associations. He is a licensed psychologist in Pennsylvania, listed in The National Register of Health Service Providers in Psychology, and is certified by the National Board of Certified Counselors. He is a member of the American Psychological Association, The Pennsylvania Psychological Association, and a past member of the Academy of Psychologists Engaged in Private Practice, Lehigh Valley.

About the Author

Dr. Zimmerman earned the bachelor of arts degree at Juniata College, Master of divinity degree at Bethany Theological Seminary, master of education, and doctor of education degrees at the Pennsylvania State University. He has completed post-doctoral studies at Duquesne University and the Pennsylvania State University.